THE PHILOSOPHY

OF

BENEDETTO CROCE

THE PHILOSOPHY OF
BENEDETTO CROCE

THE PROBLEM OF ART
AND HISTORY

BY

H. WILDON CARR
HON. D.LITT., DURHAM

NEW YORK / RUSSELL & RUSSELL

FIRST PUBLISHED IN 1917
REISSUED, 1969, BY RUSSELL & RUSSELL
A DIVISION OF ATHENEUM PUBLISHERS, INC.
BY ARRANGEMENT WITH MACMILLAN & COMPANY LTD., LONDON
L. C. CATALOG CARD NO: 69-17838
PRINTED IN THE UNITED STATES OF AMERICA

PREFACE

At the end of the volume I have given a list of Croce's principal works on Philosophy and of the English translations.

I have not made use of the English translations in the present study. My references are to the original Italian, and where I have made quotations I am entirely responsible for the rendering. In no case are the passages in quotation marks literal translations; they are freely paraphrased. What I have endeavoured to do is to understand the philosophical meaning and express it in my own manner; so much so that in many cases the quotation marks are put for reference purposes only.

English readers are deeply indebted to my friend, Mr. Douglas Ainslie, the translator of Croce's works, for his indefatigable zeal in spreading the fame of his author and obtaining recognition for the originality of his philosophy.

On one important point of terminology I find that I differ not only from Mr. Ainslie but from others who have written on Croce's philosophy, and this is not mere caprice. They use the term spirit for what I call mind.

I do not deny that there is some ground for choosing to render *lo spirito* spirit, rather than mind, inasmuch as there is a very common use of the term mind which restricts it to intellect, and *lo spirito* is more than intellect: On the other hand, I find it quite impossible to express the meaning by the word spirit, simply because to speak of an idea coming into the spirit or of an image being present to the spirit, or even to speak of the life of spirit, seems to me contrary to ordinary or desirable usage. Moreover, it seems to me that the essential doctrine of Croce is somewhat obscured by the use of the term. It is an intelligible and easily recognised doctrine that mind is reality outside which (to use a spatial expression which literally is inapplicable) there is nothing ; but it seems, to me at least, unintelligible to say that spirit is the whole of reality. When I use the term spirit it is to mark a distinction from matter. I am pleased to find that in this I am supported by the authority of the late Professor William Wallace, who has given reasons for translating *Geist* by the word Mind and not by the word Spirit (Introduction to *Hegel's Philosophy of Mind*, p. xlix).

I have not attempted to deal with all the problems which find a place in Croce's philosophical writings, nor with all the new interpretations, theoretical and practical, which his philosophy necessitates. A critical commentary on his whole work is quite outside the scope and purpose of this study. I have selected certain leading ideas which seem to me of supreme importance in the present state of philosophy.

I have to express my grateful acknowledgment to Mr. Bernard Bosanquet for the help he has given me. He read the MS., and notwithstanding that so many of the doctrines are in more or less disagreement with the doctrines expounded in his own works, especially his works on Aesthetic, his sympathetic criticisms have helped me to clear up many points which otherwise would have been left obscure or even misleading.

I have also to thank Professor J. A. Smith, whose own writings have been of great assistance to me in this work, for kindly reading the proof and giving me valuable suggestions.

I have to thank Signor Benedetto Croce for kindly sending me some of his recent addresses and contributions to Academy Journals, not easily accessible, which have been of great value to me in the elucidation of some of his theories ; also for a most useful manuscript epitome of his philosophical doctrines.

H. W. C.

September 1917.

CONTENTS

CHAPTER VIII

CHAPTER I

BENEDETTO CROCE is one of the few living philosophers who have won recognition beyond the borders of their own country. He was born in 1866. His home is in Naples. He is a Senator of the Kingdom of Italy. Possessing sufficient wealth to be full master of his time and leisure, he has devoted his life to literary and philosophical research. He rejoices that he has been able to give his mind to philosophy without the constraint a professorial appointment would have laid upon him, and a quite distinct flavour is imparted to his work by his consciousness of this freedom.

Philosophy is part only of Croce's literary activity. Literary criticism and general historical research seem to have drawn him to this field. The amount of editorial work he finds time to do is extraordinary, and bears witness to a mind overflowing with activity. He is editor of *La Critica*, a " Review of Literature, History, and Philosophy," published every two months, every number of which contains considerable contributions from his own pen. He has edited a series of translations into Italian of the classical authors of modern philosophy, and he has himself translated Hegel's *Encyclopaedia* for the series. He has also searched out and published and reanimated valuable works of authors and philosophers which had become buried in museums and public libraries. Notably he has revived the study of two great but neglected Italian philosophers, Giambattista Vico (1668–1744) and the Neapolitan patriot and literary critic, Francesco de Sanctis (1817–83). De Sanctis suffered imprisonment under the Bourbon government, 1848–52, and was afterwards first Minister of Public Instruction in the United Kingdom of Italy.

The philosophy of Croce is presented by him as a compendium and systematic classification of the mental sciences. It bears the general title *Philosophy of Mind* (*Filosofia dello Spirito*), and consists of four volumes. The first volume is entitled *Aesthetic, as Science of Expression and General Linguistic* (*Estetica, come scienza dell' espressione e linguistica generale*). It appeared in 1907 and has gone through many editions. It consists of two parts, one theoretical, the other historical. The fundamental thesis, we are told in the preface, was read before the Accademia Pontaniana of Naples at three sessions in 1900 and is included in their Proceedings. Mr. Douglas Ainslie has translated the theoretical part, and has made a summary and abstract of the historical part. The second volume is entitled *Logic as Science of the Pure Concept* (*Logica come scienza del concetto puro*). The third volume is entitled *Philosophy of Practice—Economics and Ethics* (*Filosofia della pratica—Economica ed etica*). The English translation of this by Mr. Ainslie is entitled *Philosophy of the Practical*. The fourth volume is entitled *The Theory and History of History* (*Teoria e storia della storiografia*). It has been published since my present study of the philosophy was written and while it was under revision

(1917); most of the theoretical portion, however,
consists of papers communicated to Academies and
published in their Proceedings and Essays published in
Reviews, and these I had the privilege of reading. There
are many essays and criticisms dealing with philosophy
among Croce's other writings, but these four volumes
aim at giving the complete theory in systematic form.

It is his theory of art which has brought Croce most
fame. More than any other of his doctrines it marks
out an original direction. The theory has now taken
a permanent place among rival theories of art, and is
named in the text-books *The Expressionist Theory*. Its
characteristic doctrine is that beauty is expression. The
term " expressionist " is not itself enough to characterise
the theory, and Croce is not the only philosopher who
holds that beauty is expression. But the form which he
has given to the doctrine is, I think, now generally
intended when the term is used without qualification.
The philosophical importance of the doctrine is not
merely that as an isolated theory it can claim to be freer
from intellectual difficulties than any of the many other
attempts to define the beautiful. It is something more
significant. In defining the true nature of an aesthetic
fact it indicates the place of the aesthetic activity in the
mental life. It is not a discovery in the scientific sense,
it brings to light no new fact, no new law. In itself
it may even be, so far as its mere enunciation is concerned, only a question of logical or even of grammatical
accuracy ; that is to say, all it purports to do is to
define a recognised fact of common experience. Its
value and significance, however, lie in what it implies.
This is nothing less than a new standpoint from which
with a new principle there arises a new order of knowledge and a new meaning of life and mind.

Croce presents philosophy as the science of mind. It is divided, as the science of nature is divided, into departments or groups of particular sciences, each distinguished by its subject-matter and by its special method, but no one science separate or isolated from the others, knowledge and reality being one and indivisible. The philosophical sciences are realms within the realm of mind. But the order of these sciences is not arbitrary, and the success of philosophy wholly depends on presenting the various facts of experience in their true order, the order which coincides with and represents for thought the organic unity of the individual whole.

Are there then two divisions of human knowledge, a science of nature and a science of mind ? There is but one reality, and but one science. What, then, is the principle, what the necessity of the division ? And what is the nature of the opposition between science and philosophy ?

The idea that philosophy deals with abstractions altogether removed from the vulgar realities of life, or at least that it is concerned only with problems which, however interesting as speculations, are remote from any practical issue, is not mere ignorant opinion ; it is often enough pronounced in scientific circles and even among philosophers themselves. The view that underlies it is that science deals with something peculiarly and obstinatly matter of fact, while philosophy deals with abstract notions of origin, with realities which, if they are realities, are metaphysical, in the sense that they are beyond the realm of physical inquiry and therefore beyond the sphere of positive knowledge. And many who are not actually scornful of philosophy are inclined to treat it with benevolent tolerance, as a good diversion for those who are able to acquire the taste for it.

In Croce's philosophy there is nothing transcendent in the sense that it lies beyond the sphere of positive knowledge with no relation to human life. Indeed, from the first page to the last and throughout we are invited to consider exclusively the ordinary and common-place concepts—beauty, truth, utility, and goodness— in their ordinary and commonplace meaning. What may strike the student apart from the subject-matter itself is the excessively formal treatment. There seems nothing to inspire, nothing to thrill the imagination, there are no bold speculations or brilliant hypotheses of cosmological origins or destinies ; on the contrary, most of the argument seems to be taken up with dull and at first sight unimportant and otiose inquiries. Are certain concepts true concepts or false concepts ? Are certain pretentious sciences true claimants or false? An inattentive reader might easily derive the impression that the one and only purpose of the philosopher is to classify facts in a specified order to the rejection of every other, quite apart from whether the new order is convenient or not, as though in fact it is not the matter which constitutes philosophy but only the form or framework in which the matter is arranged. We have criticisms of such sciences as rhetoric, rejections of a whole host of familiar and generally reckoned useful classifications of kinds of artistic and literary work, not as something indifferent—a mere question of con-venience or taste,—but as the very essence of philosophy. It must seem, therefore, to any one who comes to this philosophy with a mind full of awe and wonder at the mystery of the universe and intent on the great problem of life and its meaning, that so far from philosophy being high above us and hidden in cloud, it really stoops so low that it invites us to treat as matters of grave importance what to the ordinary man are trivialities.

What, then, is the distinctive note in Croce's conception of Philosophy and its place in human life? Philosophy studies the concrete, whereas science, in the sense in which that term can be opposed to philosophy, studies the abstract, and the concrete alone is real in the ultimate meaning of the term real. This is not the ordinary view, it is indeed the direct contrary of it, and probably to reach the view that reality is concrete is the hardest task the philosopher has to perform. It goes against the bent of our intellect, and the whole bias of our nature tends to contradict it. For inasmuch as with greater abstraction greater precision is attainable, and inasmuch as the ideal of all science is precision, we seem with every new abstraction to be approaching nearer the ultimate reality itself. It is illusion. The sciences increase our control of nature, they widen the range of our knowledge and therewith enlarge the sphere of our activity, they give us a deeper and more penetrating insight into reality ; but they are turned from and not towards reality itself, they take us further and further from the individual, indivisible, concrete whole which alone is actual. The abstractions which the sciences deal with, and which seem to separate themselves out as independent and isolated facts and events, and groups and classes of facts and events, have no existence and no meaning apart from the whole from which they are abstracted. On the one hand there is no limit to the process by which we abstract, and on the other hand there is no way, by mere addition, of reconstituting the whole out of which we have sorted them. If, then, science be the knowledge

of reality, there may be many abstract sciences, but
there is only one science, and that is the science of the
concrete, philosophy.

This philosophy, the science of the concrete, Croce
calls Philosophy of Mind. Mind is reality, and there
is no reality which is not mind. What are we to understand by this? Is not the science of mind an abstract
science? There is such a science of mind, an empirical
science, which like the natural sciences abstracts mental
facts from the whole as things of a special kind,
different from the class of things we call physical facts,
and from the class of things we call biological facts or
physiological facts; this is the science of psychology.
It can give us an abbreviated description and classification of the infinite facts of mind just as zoology can
abbreviate and classify the infinite varieties of living
animals. This is not the science of mind which is
Philosophy.

Is, then, this philosophy mainly and merely an idealism? Does it only insist that thoughts about things
are thoughts and not things, and that there is no passage from thoughts about things to things, no means of
escape from a subjective world of knowledge to an
objective world of independent reality? Is it only *esse*
is *percipi* once again? Or is it the doctrine that mind
makes nature? Or is it the theory that the rational is
actual and the actual rational? In some form Croce
would, I suppose, acknowledge the truth of all these
maxims, but he means something more and something
different from anything which finds expression in them.
He means that every form which reality assumes or can
assume for us has its ground within mind. There is
not and there cannot be a reality which is not mind.
This is not a manner of speaking, or a vague metaphor;

it is intended literally. This mind which is reality, or this reality which is mind, is an activity the forms of which we may distinguish ; and also we may distinguish the order and relation of the forms ; but we cannot separate them, for they are in an indissoluble organic union of dependence and interdependence on one another. Reality is a system. The work of philosophy is to present these forms of activity and show how in their processes they unite to form the concrete world of experience. Two forms of this activity we are accustomed to distinguish—knowing and acting. The first is the understanding, the theoretical activity ; the second is the will, the practical activity. They stand to one another in the relation of a definite order. Will depends on understanding in a manner in which understanding does not depend upon will. All knowing has action in view, but it is not necessary to will in order to know, and knowing does not depend on any other form of mental activity lower than itself.

We may now understand Croce's characteristic doctrine. Knowing is not a simple relation between the mind and an object independent of mind. It is not contemplation, it is an active process, and its activity has two forms, one an activity of intuition, the other an activity of conceptual thinking. The science of the one is aesthetic ; of the other, logic. Aesthetic stands to logic as a first to a second degree, for logic is dependent on aesthetic, while aesthetic depends on no other activity. The practical activity is also subdivided into an economic and an ethic activity. Knowing and acting each with its two subdivisions yield to us four pure concepts which together exhaust reality. The four pure concepts are beauty, truth, usefulness, goodness.

Let me now try and illustrate what I take to be

Croce's meaning that the concrete world is, on its theoretical side, wholly an aesthetico-logical reality. I will take an actual experience of my own with my own analysis. Suppose me, then, walking in the garden on a particular summer evening in the country. The colour is fading away as the darkness increases ; sweet scents are arising from the nocturnally fertilised flowers ; the droning of beetles, the shrill short screech of bats, as they turn rapidly in their noiseless flight, and the occasional scrunch as a chafer is caught on the wing, mingle with the distant sounds of lowing herds and the barking of a sheep-dog. As darkness deepens the stars shine out and the outlines of trees and hills gradually disappear. My thoughts as I pace silently over the lawn take a melancholy tone in pleasing harmony with the scene. This may serve as description of an experience which as experience was reality in an absolute meaning which no one is likely to question. I want to analyse not the description but the experience itself which the description serves to remind me of. I will think of it as it then was in all its infinite detail, and will try to abstract from everything in it which is in some form the mind's activity. What will be left ?

Some will be prepared with a ready answer. They will say that all that is mental is my mind's enjoyment, and that the reality itself was unaffected by this except to the extent that my presence contemplating the scene formed part of the scene. Their argument is that my presence in the garden contemplating the scene could make no difference to the reality either of me or of the scene around me, for I might have been elsewhere, and the only difference in that case would have been the absence of my enjoyment ; all else would have been what it was. Let us see.

My experience has certain easily recognisable aesthetic qualities, qualities not of my mind but of its objects. What I contemplated was beautiful. These qualities are mental. I mean that if I think of the experience as the simple, single, indivisible reality it was, not as something separable into this, that and the other, there is a quality or character of that experience which is aesthetic, and if we suppress in thought everything in the experience which is mental, we must suppress this aesthetic character. It is clearly something that cannot exist independently of mind. But the experience itself was full of imagery, was itself a composite image. This imagery was in part artistic, in part perceptual, and in each case it supposes a mental activity. We must suppress then from the experience all that is purely imaginative, whether it be artistic or perceptual. But behind this imagery, or combining and relating this imagery, there are concepts. All in the experience which enables me to classify, divide, and relate it, all that which enables me to form a scheme or diagram behind the immediate experience of a reality which I come to think the experience may represent, all this is mental. I must suppress all the logical activity which forms part of the experience. What is left when every aesthetical and every logical element or character in the experience is suppressed? Nothing is left. This I take to be the fundamental and essential position which Croce adopts in philosophy. Mind is essentially activity and mental activity is all reality.

Is there not then anything to which mind is purely passive? Let us return to the illustration of the particular experience of my own I am supposed to be analysing. I have suppressed all mental activity and nothing is left. But at least it must seem to me that there is something else, something to which I am passive, some *datum*, something given or presented to mind as the matter on which to exercise its activity. I may deny every form in which its reality can appear but I cannot suppress the thought that it must exist. What then is Croce's doctrine of this passive element? He admits it as a limiting concept, but he denies to it any positive, any concrete reality.

There are two standpoints in current philosophy in regard to this supposed necessary passive element in experience. According to one the data of sense are physical, that is non-mental, entities, and these sense-data are regarded as the real elements out of which experience is constructed. Croce's criticism of such a position would be, I think, the Kantian objection that nothing can enter experience as thing-in-itself. As experienced everything is aesthetical or logical, and aesthetic and logic are mental activities. The other standpoint is that of traditional psychology which divides experience into feelings, cognitions, and conations. It regards feelings as a purely passive class of mental entity, existing before and beneath knowing and acting. Feelings in this view are a third form of mind, neither aesthetical nor logical but prior to both. Croce wholly rejects this third form of mind, and his doctrine is in great measure based on this rejection.

Put briefly, the doctrine is that if we suppress the forms which the pure concepts beauty and truth supply, nothing remains, for the formless is not something, it is a vain attempt to conceive the inconceivable.

The view that there can be no reality external to mind is brought out with great clearness and force by Croce in the second section of the Logic which contains the doctrine of the individual judgment, and in

particular in the chapter on the predicate of existence.
" When being is conceived as external to the human
mind, and knowledge as separable from its object, so
that the object could be without being known, it is
evident that the existence of the object becomes a
datum, something, as it were, placed before the mind,
something given to the mind, extraneous to it, and
which the mind would never make its own did it not,
summoning force and courage, swallow the bitter morsel
by an irrational act of faith. And yet all philosophy,
as we go on unfolding it, shows that there is nothing
outside mind, and there are therefore no data confronting it. The very conceptions we form of this
something, which is external, mechanical, natural, show
themselves to be not conceptions of data which already
are external but data furnished to mind by itself.
Mind fashions this so-called external something because
it enjoys fashioning it, and escapes by re-annulling it
when it has no more joy in it. Moreover, no one
has yet found it possible to discover throughout the
whole range of mind the mysterious and unqualifiable
faculty it requires,—faith. It would have to be an
intuition of the universal, or a thought of the universal
without the logical process of thought. What is called
an act of faith has been shown time and again to be an
act of knowledge or an act of will, a theoretical or a
practical form of mind " (*Logica*, p. 120).

Mind, then, as philosophy teaches us to conceive it,
is a universe, which, as Leibniz said of the monad, has
no windows by means of which anything can either go
in or pass out. This is what we mean by the concreteness of reality as we study it in philosophy. All form
is given by mind and is an active process of mind, and
without form there is no reality. In philosophy we

study these forms of mental activity, not by abstracting them, not by experimenting with them, not by showing them at work *in vacuo*—we have no laboratory methods, —but by making them reveal the part they are playing in constituting the organic concrete whole. In philosophy as in life every fact is in relation with all the others, and the fact which succeeds another though different from its antecedent is yet the same. Every fact which is subsequent contains within it that which is precedent, as the precedent also contains virtually the subsequent being what it is by virtue of producing it (cf. *Logica*, p. 55).

If, then, philosophy is the science of mind, and mind includes reality, what are the sciences which we call physical and natural ? They too claim to comprehend reality, and the reality they deal with is not a different reality, for there are not two realities. " When we speak of natural *sciences* as apart from and outside of philosophy we must be careful to note that they are not *science* in the meaning we give to the term when we say philosophy is science, they are complex systems of known facts arbitrarily abstracted and fixed. The natural sciences themselves recognise that they are hedged in by limits, limits which are nothing other than historical and perceptual data. They calculate, measure, posit equations, establish regularities, fashion classes and types, formulate laws, show in a method of their own how one fact is derived from other facts, but their whole progress is a continual striving with facts intuitively and historically apprehended. Even geometry has now come to acknowledge that it rests wholly on the hypothesis that three-dimensional, or Euclidean, space is one of the possible spaces, studied preferentially because more convenient than any other. What is true in the natural sciences is either philosophy or else historical fact, what is in the true sense natural in them is abstraction and free selection. Whenever the natural sciences seek to constitute themselves perfect sciences, they are obliged to leap out of their circle and pass into philosophy. This they do when they posit concepts which are quite other than naturalistic, such as the unextended atom, the aether or vibrating medium, vital force, imperceptible space, and the like—true and fitting philosophical efforts when they are not meaningless words" (*Estetica*, p. 36).

No one can hope to follow sympathetically the exposition of Croce's ideas, if he has not first grasped the essential doctrine, not peculiar to Croce, the very ground of philosophy itself, that philosophy seeks greater concreteness, the sciences greater abstractness. It is not derogatory to the sciences, on the contrary it reveals and emphasises the value and strength of the sciences themselves. In my analysis of the experience of a summer evening, I tried to prove that, considered in its concrete integrity as individual experience, its whole nature and meaning dissolved into beauty and truth. Beauty and truth are concepts, and the science of each is the science of a mental activity, one aesthetic and the other logical, and if there be anything outside these concepts it can only be a kind of sense-material to which mind has not yet given form,—data, not in any sense extra-mental, but abstracted from their form in the mental apprehension, an attempt to conceive rather than a conception. But it may be said it is not the reality or unreality of unformed sense-matter that we are ever in the least concerned about. What we want to discover is the physical reality of physical things, and we mean by physical things not our experience, but the proximate cause of experience. It is obvious that if we could be satisfied with the reality of our experience—a reality never in doubt—then the problem of physical reality would not arise. It is equally obvious that it is human nature not to be satisfied with immediate experience, that it is experience itself which drives us to seek, by reflexion on it, its ground or source. And, once again, it is obvious that if we follow this bent of our nature, the process must be directed, in the first place at least, away from and not towards reality. And we find, in fact, that both philosophy and the sciences use immediate experience as a jumping-off ground in the search for reality.

I *experienced* that summer evening in the garden, but I shall not *understand* it unless my mind can pass beyond it. There are two ways, contrary in their direction, by which I may seek to pass beyond the actual experience. They both imply that the experience itself is hedged round and marked off by purely arbitrary and conventional limits. I may seek to fit my experience into a greater whole. What meaning or character can that summer evening possess which it does not owe to my whole individual experience, and even to a larger experience than that, an experience which transcends the individual and embraces the race? In replacing my experience within the whole from which I have arbitrarily hedged it off, I sacrifice nothing of its reality, but I find the ground of its reality in a richer, more concrete, whole. This is the way of philosophy. But my mind is also drawn in another direction. I classify, and separate, and abbreviate my experience. In distinguishing and concentrating attention on single points of interest within an experience and neglecting all others, I seem to acquire a more and more definite and precise view of the conditions which lie' behind the experience as its ground. I do not proceed arbitrarily and at random, I follow definite principles of interpretation, and I find the ground of my experience, or of any distinguishing feature in it, in an entirely new and different order. This is the way of the sciences. Their success is stupendous. Yet the reality they have given me is an unreality, the condition is always simpler and more abstract than the conditionate, and consequently falls short somewhere of full reality. On the other hand, the reality philosophy gives me is an ideality, something more and not less than the experience of which it is the ground.

It is sometimes argued that the higher facts of mind only present a more complex, not a different problem, from that which is afforded by the apparition of new qualities, in the world ; when, for example (to take the simple and often used illustration), the gaseous elements oxygen and hydrogen combine and form water. It is instructive, however, to consider the inverse of the argument. The word " water " may bring to mind an almost infinite variety of experience ; it will awaken ideas of lakes, oceans, rain, cloud, snow, ice, moisture, dryness, thirst, cleansing, etc., in any wealth of detail. If I am a chemist I have by means of classifying and abbreviating reduced all this variety to a simple formula, I say that two atoms of hydrogen are combined with one of oxygen. Plainly my formula, on the value of which there is no need to insist, indicates one very abstract property of the infinitely varied phenomena which I know as water, and starting from that property alone, supposing it could come first in the order of knowing, I should never pass to the richness of the full reality.

The most striking instance of the principle, however, is found in the mathematical conceptions of space and time, for in these we reach the limit óf abstractness with, at the same time, the most absolute basis of physical reality. "The whole conception of things," Croce observes at the conclusion of the second section of the *Logic*, "as occupying various positions of space, and succeeding in a discontinuous manner, one thing detached from another in time, is an alteration, which has been effected for practical ends, of the ingenuous view presented to pure perception." "The mathematical concepts of space and time are excogitations of abstractness not to be confused with real thinking, the genuine thinking of reality. The same conclusion is affirmed in the Kantian concept of the ideality of time and space, a doctrine which is among the greatest philosophical discoveries in history, and which every philosophy, which is truly such, must accept. In accepting it myself, I only make the reservation that this character of mathematical space and time ought not to be termed ideality (for ideality is the true reality) but rather unreality or abstract ideality or, as I prefer to say, abstractness" (*Logica*, p. 137).

I have tried to show by the analysis of an actual experience that when those constituents of the experience which probably every one would agree to regard as mental are suppressed, there is no remainder. Further, I have suggested that the apparent independent existence of a basis or material substratum of the experience is due to the practical manner in which we organise our experience by abstracting its constituents and classifying them. I do not claim, however, that this analysis, even if it be accepted, settles the problem of the nature and origin of sense-experience. For one thing, it does not show us why sense-experience is individual experience. Indeed I am only too conscious that it carries us but a short step on the way to a philosophy of mind. That preliminary step is, however, of quite fundamental importance. It enables us to recognise at the outset that in all cognitive experience mind is immanent as active process, itself giving objective form to knowledge. Mind does not stand in a transcendent relation to an extraneous object which it passively contemplates. But now I may be asked, do I mean that I myself invent or create my experience? Are those products of mental activity—images and concepts—the work of the individual mind? If not, then what is the relation of the existing individual mind to the universal reality, mind? In this question the whole problem of philosophy opens out before us. Even though mind be identical with reality, unless I am (what no one has been or can be) a consistent solipsist, there is reality confronting me which does not owe its nature or existence to my aesthetical and logical activity.

A complete answer is the complete philosophy, but I will indicate at once the particular way in which it seems to me Croce's theory meets this problem. It is in the concept of history. Every individual mind is a history; and illimitable history exists in every actual active mental process. The individual mind therefore carries along with it, in its aesthetical and logical inventiveness, a past which is itself determined in the present and which is also itself eternally determining the present. The reality, therefore, which confronts the individual mind is history, and with history the individual mind is identical. I shall deal with this problem in its place, I only indicate now the direction in which its solution is to be sought.

There is yet another question which will force itself upon us in this connexion. What is the nature of the plurality of individuals? Are individuals eddies in an ocean of universal mind? Or are they monads, each developing its individual nature on an internal principle of evolution, each secured by that nature against intrusion or effective influence from without?

I do not know that there is any direct attempt to deal with this problem in Croce's work, such as would enable me to give his answer in his own words, but it certainly seems to me that his aesthetic doctrine that intuition is expression tends to a monadic view. The real solution, however, I believe, is to be looked for, in regard to this problem also, in the concept of history. The history which has produced the individual mind, which constitutes its nature and determines the form of its existence has also produced the common nature, or as we say of ourselves, the human nature. Therefore it is that the world of our cognition is a human world, and we must suppose that for the dog there is a canine world, and for an angel, if there be angels, an angelic world. But in this reflexion it is possible that I may be only intruding a view of my own.

The concrete life of mind is, then, in Croce's view, the subject-matter of the Science which is philosophy. By concreteness is meant the full reality of mind as it manifests itself in its historical development. Let us now consider the concept of life which it involves. The life of mind is not a biological concept, nor is it a metaphysical concept. It is a historical concept, or rather we ought to say it is the concept of history. This brings us, therefore, to the striking and distinguishing characteristic of Croce. He holds that philosophy is not an ontology but a methodology.

This is Croce's own term, but it is hardly likely to convey his meaning without explanation, for he uses it in a wider and somewhat different sense than that to which we are accustomed. He means that philosophy is a science of order and arrangement, and not a metaphysic or science of a noumenal reality beyond the phenomenal world of ordinary fact and historical event. Croce holds that it is not the business of philosophy to attempt to solve the riddle of the universe or to unveil its mystery. Life for him is not the principle of existence but the reality manifesting itself in activity, a reality to be accepted, not deduced. The method of philosophy is not transcendent but immanent, for we cannot by thought pass outside the life of mind which has no limits, no beyond. Philosophy cannot put us at the beginning of history nor embrace the whole of history within a concept. History has no finality. And, again, we cannot understand this life by formulating the *a priori* conditions of its possibility. On the other hand, by methodology Croce intends something very different from what is ordinarily meant by that word. It usually stands for a conception of philosophy like that of positivism—the concept of a science of the sciences. Croce means by it that philosophy is one with history, and history one with philosophy. The life of mind is revealed in action, and the interpretation of action is history. A mere narration of events arbitrarily selected and formally recorded is not philosophy, but also it is not history. History is a judgment on events, and the historical judgment and the philosophical judgment are identical. Methodology is the science of the formation of the historical judgment, and the full technical description of it is methodology of historiography.

By saying that philosophy is methodology, not meta-

physics, Croce does not mean to debase philosophy nor
to exclude from it any branch or any aspect of human
knowledge, empirical or speculative. On the contrary
he claims that his conception of philosophy exalts it
above every other. Metaphysics cannot solve its own
problems without giving an imaginative and arbitrary
form to its doctrines, but methodology by criticising
and revealing the genesis of the metaphysical problems
can resolve those as well as the problems peculiarly its
own. The reality of the external world, the soul substance, the unknowable, the antinomies, all the problems
which metaphysics has sought to resolve, are completely
altered when the new and better concepts of a theory of
knowledge show these questions to be eternal aspects of
knowledge, eternally overcome by the dialectic and
phenomenology of knowledge itself.

Croce denies, therefore, that there is any fundamental problem of philosophy or any particular character
marking a man out as a philosopher. The figure of the
holy Buddha, or of the monk, or of the sage, who has
turned aside from mundane affairs to contemplate the
mystery of existence, he rejects together with the concept of philosophy as especially a theological or metaphysical science. He would introduce a new concept
of philosophy identifying it with the study of history in
that full meaning in which history is the interpretation
of life. So he would bring philosophy from heaven to
earth, and make it speak the language and think the
thoughts of ordinary humanity.

"When we think of the psychological observations
and moral doubts which poetry, romance, and drama,
the voices of our society, have accumulated, in the
course of the nineteenth century alone, and consider
that these are for the most part still without critical

elaboration, we may form some idea of the great tasks which stand waiting for philosophy to undertake. And when, without looking back on the past, we consider only the multitude of anxious inquiries raised on every side by the present war—concerning the state, concerning history, right, the duties of peoples, civilisation, culture, barbarism, science, art, religion, the end and ideal of life, and so forth—we see clearly how it behoves philosophers to come out of the theologico-metaphysical circle, in which they remain shut up even when impatient of the very mention of theology and metaphysics, since, notwithstanding the new concept they have adopted and professed, their mind and intellect are still orientated toward the old ideas" (*Teoria della Storiografia*, p. 147).

This tendency to identify philosophy with history and to reject the theological and metaphysical problems, or at least to subordinate them to the problem of the historical judgment, is, to a certain extent, a personal trait of Benedetto Croce himself. His own interest, the interest which has drawn him to philosophy and immersed him in its problems, is not scientific, nor is it religious, but artistic and literary. He is not a mathematician, or a physicist, or a biologist, or a priest, or a professor, and the problems presented by science and religion have not the overpowering interest for him which they possess for those engaged in scientific researches and religious duties. Hence the humanist tone of his thought and bent of his theories.

CHAPTER II

PHILOSOPHY of Mind, Croce tells us, is anti-metaphysical and methodological. Such a view may seem at once to place him in antagonism not only to the main tendency of present philosophical research, but also to the historical philosophical tradition. It is important, therefore, to understand exactly what is meant.

There are two ways in which we may regard the relation of philosophy to science. We may distinguish the subject-matter with which philosophy deals from that with which science deals. One way of marking this distinction is the popular one expressed in the terms physics and metaphysics. Physics is regarded as the realm of positive science, but this realm is not marked off by a sharply defined boundary line. It is limited by a sort of conceptual boundary within which is a zone of what is clearly known, or of what is capable of being clearly known, and beyond is the unknown, some think the unknowable, which they regard as an x whose existence we may postulate. This beyond is the realm of metaphysics. Metaphysics, because it is beyond physics and therefore not amenable to laboratory methods, is not necessarily on that account a realm of knowledge which is indefinite, obscure or confused, for it may be amenable to other methods. Philosophical method may be as rigorous, as firm, and as sure as that of physical science, but it deals with quite other questions, with the ultimate questions which concern the ground or source of scientific reality. It does not deal with reality in so far as it is accessible to science.

There is another way of regarding the relation. In this we make no distinction whatever between realms of reality, it is one and the same reality which we study in science and in philosophy. The distinction is wholly in the method. Philosophy studies reality in its concreteness ; physical science studies it in its abstractness. Scientific method is a method of isolating and separating from its place in the whole scheme, certain aspects of reality, or certain systems of reality, and it takes for granted that the facts thus abstracted are unaltered by their abstraction from the full reality ; an assumption which philosophy challenges.

These two ways of regarding the relation of philosophy to science are not mutually exclusive. Both point to something in the special function of philosophy which every philosopher would acknowledge to be true. The difference between philosophers is not in their rejection of the one and acceptance of the other so much as in the emphasis with which they accentuate the function of philosophy. It is this emphasis on the metaphysical function of philosophy on the one hand or on the methodological function on the other, rather than disagreement as to the purpose and scope of philosophy which gives distinct character to an individual philosopher.

In one sense an anti-metaphysical philosophy is a contradiction in terms. There are many who deny, some with vehemence, the possibility of metaphysics. When this denial is based on demonstration, those of us who profess ourselves metaphysicians, have to hail these deniers as fellow-metaphysicians, for they are announcing and defending a very definite metaphysical theory, negative though it be. A considered denial of metaphysics is therefore, as Descartes discovered in the case of his principle *cogito ergo sum*, a confirmation of the existence of what it would deny. But let us set aside this extreme case and examine what is implied positively when philosophy is identified with metaphysics.

A metaphysical philosophy implies that in some form we distinguish a world of reality from a world of appearance ; a noumenal from a phenomenal world ; mind, or spirit, or God, from external nature ; life or freedom from mechanism. It implies further that this reality which we may now term metaphysical may be studied independently of the world of common-sense experience and physical science, that is, as another, and different world. The two worlds are of course not thought of as cut off and separate from one another, but they are as different in their nature as the world of the Ideas or intellectual forms was different from the world of shadows to the men in the den, in Plato's allegory.

This view of philosophy may be described as that which makes it the science of the other world. In whatever form we meet it, it is the effort of the mind to transcend the world of nature, art, and history, and to transport itself into another world. It may be an effort to ascend into a supra-world, or it may be an effort to neglect, or abstract from, the conditions of space and time in order to obtain a vision of a reality *sub specie aeternitatis*. In popular imagination the philosopher is devoted to this task. Like Teufelsdröck in Carlyle's *Sartor Resartus* he must strip off the garments which convention has woven around his life, strip off the flesh garment which nature has bestowed upon him, strip off the space and time garment which confine his outlook to a particular here and now, in order that he may see himself as he really is.

Quite different is Croce's view of the purpose and scope and justification of philosophy. The method of philosophy is in his view immanent and not transcendent. And it is in its immanence that it is in complete antithesis to the method of science. Philosophy is the science of reality, and reality is one and indivisible, but philosophy studies reality in its concrete integrity, and from within as the unfolding of an ideal history. For philosophy, therefore, reality is mind and mind is reality. But mind is not a thing among other things, it is for philosophy the all-embracing reality ; there is no reality other than mind. Philosophy organises knowledge on a principle altogether different from that which physical science follows. It seeks to determine the moments of a continuous, ideal unfolding or development. The philosophical sciences, Aesthetic, Logic, Economics, and Ethics, are not abstract sciences, or co-ordinated systems of independent facts, they are grades, or degrees, or moments, in the active life of mind. This principle of an immanent or indwelling knowledge as distinct from a transcendent knowledge, if it be termed anti-metaphysical, is equally and at the same time anti-positivist. It is not an abandonment of metaphysics in the sense in which the Comtists meant it. Metaphysics is not for Croce a stage in the emancipation of the human mind marking its progress from mythology and theology to the clear light of positivism. No co-ordination and no hierarchy of the mathematical and natural sciences can yield a philosophy. Positivism as a method is empirical, not transcendent ; but also it is not immanent, it is external.

In declaring philosophy to be anti-metaphysical Croce means not a condemnation of metaphysics but a protest against identifying philosophy with metaphysics. It is not a special direction of research nor is it a particular line of speculation which makes a man a philosopher ; he is a philosopher by virtue of his human nature. It is as fundamental a need of that nature to know reality in the way of philosophy as it is to know it in the way of science. All men are philosophers, some are philosophical giants, some are philosophical dwarfs.

On the other hand, philosophy is not, and cannot be, identified with the mathematical and physical sciences, and these sciences are not, as Comte taught, a series or ascending scale of degrees which philosophy comes to complete and to crown. Neither is philosophy an order discovered in or imposed upon the various groups of facts which the sciences classify and systematise; nor is science as represented by these special systems a co-ordinate method with the method of philosophy. Philosophy, as science of mind or of spirit, differs from the sciences of physics or nature, in precisely the same meaning in which common sense contrasts mind and body, spirit and matter, consciousness and nature. With this important proviso, however, that for any one who regards mind, spirit, consciousness, whichever of these terms is chosen to denote reality in its spiritual aspect, as a thing among things, a partial reality, or a part of reality, philosophy does not exist. Philosophy for such a one will be psychology, and psychology will then take its place among the special sciences. So we speak of the *philosophy* of mind and of the *science* of nature, and in this contrast between philosophy and science we present two modes of apprehending reality each of which exhausts reality. Philosophy and science are not rivals nor are they brother monarchs holding rule over different realms ; they stand to one another in the wholly unique relation that for philosophy, reality or mind is concrete, the whole ; for science, reality or nature is abstract, a partial aspect. Philosophy is therefore the Science of sciences.

It seems to me that this idea of a new philosophy which is anti-metaphysical and anti-positivist is in perfect harmony with the highest philosophical effort in the thought of to-day and with the noblest tradition of the philosophy of the past. Yet it is a new departure and it is a revolution. It may not startle us with its novelty, it may not appear as a revolutionary innovation. It proposes, in fact, that we shall begin and organise philosophy on the same model on which the thought of the Western nations has so successfully organised physical science. It declares that we can know this present world philosophically as well as scientifically.

This distinction between philosophy and science, between knowing philosophically and knowing scientifically, is a quite modern distinction. It did not exist for the ancient philosophy, and it did not exist for modern philosophy when it arose in the seventeenth century. It marks a dichotomy which became particularly pronounced in the latter half of the nineteenth century, owing to the enormous advance of economic or applied science. It emphasises a direction of the mind determined by inductive and experimental research. It has given definite meaning to the word " scientist." By scientist we have come to denote one who regards reality as external to mind, fixed and static, not excluding dynamism or the concept of energy, but explaining all activity as external movement. By philosopher we have come to mean one who regards reality as a history, not necessarily as a time process, but essentially as an internal activity which manifests itself outwardly, and which we usually name life or mind.

There is however another distinction, one which is more fundamental and which attaches to philosophy from the beginning and throughout its whole history. It may be summed up as the antithesis between reason and authority. It is this distinction which, if I interpret him rightly, Croce has in mind throughout his polemic against a metaphysical philosophy.

It is a commonplace of historical criticism that the rise of modern philosophy in the seventeenth century was a new birth. Philosophy had been dead for the greater part of the two thousand years which separated the modern enlightenment heralded by Descartes' *Discours de la Méthode* from the Greek successors of Aristotle. But throughout this whole period there had never been any lack of what called itself philosophy. Metaphysics flourished and flourished exuberantly. It is usual to say that philosophy suffered eclipse or was stifled by the baneful influence of theology. But theology was metaphysics in the true Aristotelian meaning of the term—the science of what is beyond physics. The general criticism of theology is that it relies on authority and is based ultimately on faith in the truth of a revelation, but this is merely incidental, what is essential to it is the otherness of the world to which it introduces us. The real world of theology stands to the common-sense world of experience and science in the relation of ground to consequence, but the ground is presented as another and different world.

Modern philosophy has from the first, and as its distinguishing character, divested itself of all reliance on authority, and has asserted the self - sufficiency of reason, but it has not divested itself of this other-world concept. This still clings to philosophers who have emancipated themselves from every trace of theological prepossession. Let us get rid of it finally and absolutely is the burden of Croce's plea for an anti-metaphysical philosophy.

How then would Croce re-organise philosophy ? There are, I think, two leading principles of his re-organisation. They concern the one, art, the other, history. He insists that aesthetic is to be studied, not as a detached and transcendent human interest, but as an integral part of reality. And further, he insists that philosophy is identical with history. Let us consider each of these principles.

The first step to a re-organisation of philosophy is the inclusion of aesthetic and the assignment to it of its right place in the life of mind. With this is bound up the recognition of the importance of theory of art, important because art is one chief domain of human activity. So insistent is Croce in pressing the claims of theory of art on philosophers that he tends to identify the problem it presents with philosophy itself.

It is necessary in studying Croce to bear this direction of his interest continually in mind. Every philosopher comes to philosophy with some preponderating interest — it may be the problem of religion, the problem of biology, the problem of physical reality, the problem of good and evil, but according to his interest the direction and form of his speculation is determined. There is no such thing as disinterested philosophy, for we who philosophise are

human beings and our activity is itself the reality we
are concerned to know.   Philosophy therefore moves
from within outwards, and it is not the dispassionate
view of a spectator who has neither part nor lot in
what he beholds.

Aesthetic, then, in Croce's view, is an integral part
of philosophy, but its claim to be so considered is com-
paratively recent.   It arose when modern philosophy
arose in the seventeenth century and has advanced *pari
passu* with the advance of philosophy.   The aesthetic
problem has been in fact the driving force in the whole
development of modern philosophy.   For Descartes
and his successors in the seventeenth century, for
Leibniz and his successors in the eighteenth century,
the aesthetic problem took the form of the relation
to one another of two mental faculties which they
distinguished by the terms imagination and intellect.
The one was the source of obscure and confused
knowledge, the other of clear and distinct ideas.   It
was this distinction which determined the development
of philosophy towards intellectualism.   The obscure
and confused knowledge, the origin of error and
illusion, was the knowledge we obtain through the
senses ; the clear and distinct ideas were the ideas of
the intellect pure from sensuous elements.   But this
sensible knowledge, aesthetic, this fruitful source of
deception, must have some purpose ; also it must have
a ground of its existence.   The theory which found
favour was that it stood for a lower relation, the
relation of mind to body, while the intellect pointed
to a higher relation, the union of the mind with God.
The senses were not given to us, so at least the
Cartesians held, in order that we might acquire knowledge, but in order to serve as a protection to our body.

" If you would have me discourse on my meta-physical visions, my dear Ariston, we must leave this pleasant surrounding with so much to charm the senses for it distracts a mind like mine. Let us retire within your chamber where we may shut out distrac-tions and permit the intellect to work undisturbed, for I am apprehensive lest I mistake for immediate deliverance of inner truth, some of my own prejudices, or some of those confused principles which owe their existence to the laws of the union of soul and body. Let us endeavour to consult universal reason only, our common master, for it is inner truth which must preside over our discourse." Thus Malebranche opens the first of his *Entretiens sur la Métaphysique*, and therein he speaks as the typical and representative philosopher. But is it not evident, at least to us now looking back over the course of modern philosophy, that in thus restricting himself, the philosopher is actually turning his face away from reality and adopting a method which makes its attainment impossible? He is shutting out nine-tenths of life, and the tenth he retains is transformed and worthless by reason of its abstractness from the whole reality. But the old proverb *naturam expelles furca* is illustrated here also. The world of sense has too strong a claim on our attention, it will assert itself despite our utmost efforts to discredit it. If philosophy can find no place for aesthetic, if it despise it and reject it as unworthy, a region of confused and turbid knowledge, aesthetic will grow up in its own way out-side a philosophy hypnotised by metaphysics. And this is what in effect did happen. Aesthetic arose in the seventeenth century born of the same travail of the human mind which brought forth philosophy.

" The problem which, more or less consciously,

occupied the professors and students of rhetoric and
the art critics in the seventeenth century, notably in
Italy, consequent on the disputes and literary reflec-
tions of the preceding century, was the discovery and
distinction of special faculties. They distinguished a
faculty for the production of art which they termed
'genius.' It differed from mere intellect, being more
especially inventive and creative of beauty, and they
affiliated it to imagination or fantasy. They further
distinguished a faculty of judging art, different from
syllogistic reasoning, which they named 'judgment'
or 'taste' and affiliated sometimes to feeling, sometimes to the intuition or discernment of something
indefinable. During this same period Descartes and
his immediate successors, struck with wonder at the
amenability of human knowledge to mathematical
evidence, ignored or rejected what seemed to them to
be turbid modes of thinking and judging. For the
greater glory of Reason they suppressed imagination,
and sacrificed poetry to mathematics and metaphysics.
And yet we cannot say that Descartes was retrogressive
compared with those who meditated on genius, taste,
feeling, the indefinable somewhat, nor that they were
retrogressive compared with Descartes. The two
problems were different ; they originated in truths
which are distinct. The one was the outcome of the
attempts to discover the part which poetry and art
play in the mental life ; the other founded, in ration-
alistic form, a philosophy of mind which was absolutely
necessary if discoveries were to be set free from initial
uncertainty and precariousness."

"The new problem which emerged with Leibniz
was the unity of these two movements. He combined
in himself the truth of both. He found a place in

his theory of knowledge for the confused cognitions which precede the distinct and clear cognitions, for the poetry which precedes philosophy. His pupils drew directly from it a body of doctrine, a special science, *Scientia cognitionis sensitivae, ars analogi rationis, gnoseologia inferior,* which they baptized with the name ' Aesthetic ' " (*Inizio, Periodi e Carattere della Storia dell' Estetica,* paper read to the Accademia Pontaniana, November 5, 1916).

Let us now look at the other principle which I have said underlies Croce's idea of a new philosophy. This is the essential identity of philosophy and history. The philosopher and the historian are engaged on one and the same task, namely, the interpretation of present existing fact. The goal and the inspiring ideal in the research which each undertakes is the bringing to the light of clear consciousness the inner system of reality hidden from us in practical life by the outward show. This revelation or unveiling of the system of reality has two moments, which we name respectively theory and history, and which correspond to the distinction of nature and genesis in every fact of experience. They are different moments in one identical process ; now one, now the other, is emphasised. Philosophy comes to be attached to the moment of theory and so to be distinguished from the moment of history. It is noticeable that throughout his own work Croce keeps closely to a historical method. He philosophises as a historian and he writes history as a philosopher. Every new problem in philosophy, every concept which marks an advance in philosophical theory is evolved historically and can only be philosophically interpreted by a reflection on its history.

" Philosophy is an elucidation of the directive concepts of historical interpretation. Since the subject of history is the concrete life of mind and since life consists in imagination and thought, in action and morality, and yet is one throughout the variety of its forms, the elucidation works of itself in the distinctions of aesthetic and logic, of economics and ethics, and all are conjoined and resolved in the Philosophy of Mind. If a philosophical problem be shown by the historical judgment to be sterile in fact, by that alone it is proved to be otiose or at any rate out of place and without real subsistence. If a philosophical proposition, instead of making history more intelligible, leave it obscure or in worse confusion, or if it leap above history or condemn and deny it, this would itself be proof that the proposition and the philosophy bound up in it is arbitrary, however interesting as a mani-festation of feeling and fantasy " (*Critica*, vol. xvi. p. 308).

In denouncing metaphysical philosophy, Croce is not then, it seems to me, denouncing metaphysics. No doubt he considers very much current metaphysics to be otiose, but his main protest is against other-world science, and his main purpose is to identify philo-sophy with art and with history. Philosophy is not a refuge from time and appearance.

It may be said perhaps that other - worldness characterises physical science in as marked and definite a meaning as it characterises metaphysical philosophy, yet no one would discredit science on that account. Atoms, molecules, electrons, aether, and the new mathematical hypotheses of a constant velocity and a variable space and time, introduce us to a world which is other than the world of sensible experience, precisely as the timeless world, the *species aeternitatis* of the philosopher is other than the world of historical events. The analogy, however, is only in externals. Physical and mathematical hypotheses and theories are not offered to the mind as another world which we enter only in so far as we transcend experience, they do not profess to enable us to pass beyond or behind the world of experience, what they do is to construct for us a schematic system by which we are able to give mechanical completeness to the concept of external nature which is the necessary condition of our practical activity. This scientific construction has purely economic value.

Let us turn now to the positive aspect of this idea of an anti-metaphysical philosophy. If we agree in rejecting metaphysics in the meaning of other-worldness, what is the scope and purpose of philosophy ? What is its character ? In what way is it to be organised and systematised ?

Philosophy, as we have seen, is the study of mind in its concrete activity, not as a thing among things, but in its life, and this life of mind is the whole of reality. This means that for philosophy all distinctions such as mental and non-mental, psychical and physical, spirit and matter, sign and thing signified, existence and meaning, fall within philosophy and do not serve to distinguish an accessible reality from an inaccessible reality or thing-in-itself. Mind is full concrete reality and philosophy studies it in its concreteness. There is no fundamental problem of philosophy in the static sense, no riddle of existence, the solution of which has to be sought. Successive systems of philosophy are not guesses at truth nor are they well-intentioned attempts to throw light on an unchanging problem.

The problem of philosophy is ever-changing because mind is living activity and change is of its essence. Philosophy therefore is history, history which on the one hand is ideal, the development or unfolding of life as the activity of an inner principle ; and on the other hand is external, the continued advance from what is acted to what is acting. Philosophy is consciousness of reality as immanent, that is as subjective, an indwelling activity expressing itself in its expanding life. It conceives reality immanent in mind. It is to be clearly distinguished from the pantheistic conception of a mind immanent in nature ; for pantheism, it is nature which is transcendent. Another way of stating the doctrine is to say that reality for philosophy is essentially and wholly subjective, objectivity being an aspect of it or an abstract view of it.

If we accept this conception we shall at once see that the problems of philosophy will be multifarious, and that however we may decide to arrange or group them, it will be now one group and now another which will come to the front and seem fundamental. So we come to divide the actual, that is, the external, history of philosophy into periods, each of which is marked by the prominence of some problem or group of problems, which ever tends to grow in complexity until finally it gives place to a new group of problems. There is no finality, because reality is itself not static or finite, not something to be discovered once and for all, but continuous life. The solution of the philosophical problems which are exercising our generation will not issue in a body of doctrine finally acceptable for all generations to come ; the only solution they will have will be that they will bring to view new problems for new generations to solve.

The outstanding feature in contemporaneous philosophy is in Croce's view the inclusion of aesthetic in philosophy and the recognition of aesthetic, as a distinct moment in the ideal history of the life of mind. And he finds this illustrated in the external history of aesthetic and in the development of its relation to philosophy, beginning with its rise in the seventeenth century. He distinguishes four periods. The first is that of the aesthetic before Kant, when the leading motive was the search for an aesthetic "faculty," and the determination of its place among the other "faculties" of the mind. The second is the aesthetic of Kant and his successors which exhausted itself in metaphysical idealism, in which the "faculties" of the mind lost their character of abstractness, and were no longer represented as in juxtaposition, but came to mean the ideal history of the mind. And in this ideal progression art found a place, though still regarded as a kind of religious epic, religion itself having become a myth more or less aesthetic. The third period is that of positivism and psychology which continued almost to the end of the nineteenth century. In this there is a reaction against the metaphysics of art and a return to the consideration of art as naturalistic. It does not reach a theory of art, yet it achieves something, for it marks the healthy rejection of metaphysical disquisition in aesthetic. The fourth period is that of contemporary aesthetic, which, now free from metaphysics and from positivism, but not from philosophy, is resuming the study of the problems of art in the form of a philosophy of the aesthetic mind.

Apart from this special interest of aesthetic, how does this concept of anti-metaphysical philosophy affect the general problem of life and knowledge? To most of

those who are familiar with the history of thought, the idea
of a new philosophy anti-metaphysical and anti-positivist
will probably bring to mind Kant's question discussed
in the *Prolegomena*, " Is metaphysics possible at all ? "
together with the negative conclusion he reached on
the ground that there is no knowledge of things-in-
themselves. To those, however, who think they perceive
that reality is not a thing, something static, but the
living change itself in its concrete activity, the question
in the form in which Kant propounded it is devoid
of meaning. In thinking and in acting we know
reality, and other reality there is none to know. We
who take this view recognise no things, independent
of our thinking and doing, supporting the reality we
contemplate and change. Our philosophy is then not
a metaphysics but a methodology, a mode of knowing
which apprehends this active life of mind in its concreteness and not in its abstractness, and which apprehends it from within as immanent reality or life and
not from without as transcendent reality or thing-in-
itself.

CHAPTER III

THE word "aesthetic" in philosophy is used in two connexions which seem to be distinct, or perhaps we should rather say, it serves to denote two kinds of facts which seem to have nothing in common. It is used to describe those qualities of objects, or those aspects of nature and art, which draw from us admiration, or give us pleasure, on account of their beauty. We call these the aesthetic qualities, and we regard them as quite different from those qualities of things which constitute their physical reality and also from those qualities which make them objects of desire. The satisfaction beauty gives us is of another kind, we feel, to that which we derive from the agreeableness or the goodness of objects. This is the use of the word aesthetic which corresponds to its meaning in ordinary, non-technical, discourse. When we apply the terms aesthetic, aestheticism, to persons or things, we mean cultivation of taste and appreciation of beauty.

There is also another and more technical use of the word to denote not merely the qualities we judge to be beautiful but qualities which are perceptual in distinction from those which are conceptual or ideal. This corresponds to a very ancient philosophical distinction between the things of sense and the things of thought. It might be very useful to have words to denote this distinction, and we might translate the Greek words and speak of aestheta and noëta, or else use purely English equivalents, and speak of sensibles and intelligibles. It is a distinction, however, which, though important in philosophical analysis, is rarely required in ordinary discourse.

These two uses of the term " aesthetic " appear to have nothing in common, unless it be the mere fact that sensible or perceptual elements form the basis of all knowledge and therefore also of aesthetic qualities in the first meaning. Indeed the two meanings often seem to be opposite or contrary to one another in their application, or at least to apply the one to the very lowest sphere of mental activity, the other to the very highest.

Nowhere is this more clearly illustrated than in the philosophy of Kant. One great critique, the *Critique of Judgment*, is devoted by Kant to the aesthetic problem in the first meaning of the term, namely to the knowledge of the beautiful and the sublime. It is the third of the great critiques, and was evidently regarded by him as concerned with the most exalted of the powers of the mind. The *Critique of Pure Reason* had dealt with the faculty of cognition ; the *Critique of Practical Reason* with the faculty of desire ; Judgment, the faculty dealt with in the third critique, is that which constitutes finality or purpose. This faculty of Judgment is in Kant's phraseology the *a priori* condition of the feeling of pleasure and displeasure. The beautiful and the sublime he held to be the objects of a satisfaction quite distinct from those which give us the satisfaction of truth and the satisfaction of goodness. Aesthetic qualities are distinguished from, and raised

above, all others by their character of disinterestedness
and universality. They are disinterested, for the satisfaction we derive from a beautiful object is impersonal,
it is not agreeableness or goodness. They are universal,
for when we judge a thing beautiful we mean not
merely that it is to our taste but that it is beautiful to
all beholders. The basis of the aesthetic judgment
Kant held to be the discernment of end or purpose,
and its highest attainment was to become the symbol
of the moral good. Aesthetic was therefore for Kant
the highest realm of the activity of the mind.

Kant also used the term "aesthetic" to indicate a
mental activity of a quite lower order, even the lowest
order of all. The "Transcendental Aesthetic" of the
first part of the *Critique of Pure Reason* deals with the
first work of the mind in constituting our knowledge
of nature. Before the understanding can receive into
its frames the perceptual matter of knowledge, this
perceptual matter must itself have received the perceptual form. This the mind supplies through the
senses themselves by means of the *a priori* forms of
space and time. This first activity, the apprehending
of reality under perceptual form, is named by Kant
aesthetic, although it seems to have had in his theory
no relation to the aesthetic judgment of the sublime
and beautiful. It was exhausted in giving to the
chaos of sense its primitive relational unity in the
forms of space and time. Much and very different
work separated this activity from the higher one, and
had to be done before the conditions could be realised
in which the human mind could say not only this is
true and this is good, but also, this is beautiful.

In Croce's philosophy Aesthetic is the science of
the mental activity which gives us knowledge of the

beautiful ; but, unlike Kant, Croce holds that this knowledge is not the highest attainment of the human mind, on the contrary, it is the lowest of all. It is lowest, not in the sense that it is least worthy, but that it is the first grade on which all other grades of activity depend. Our knowledge of truth and our knowledge of goodness depend upon, and in that sense only are higher than, our knowledge of beauty. Croce accordingly places the aesthetic activity in the same position as that to which Kant assigned the "Trans- cendental Aesthetic" in the *Critique of Pure Reason*, but then, unlike Kant, he does not confine this activity to the apprehension of experience under the forms of space and time, indeed he denies that aesthetic appre- hension is always or necessarily spatial and temporal.

It may seem a matter of small moment whether the Aesthetic activity is higher or lower than another activity, where all are equally necessary and where none can exist separately from the mental life in which they form an organic unity. In fact, however, the whole possibility of a true theory of the nature of the aesthetic activity depends on the place we assign to it in the mental life.

There is an immense literature on the subject of art and theory of art, but probably in regard to no other subject of the same importance is there more confusion and more direct contradiction as to the nature of the elementary fact upon which the subject is based. To most people art is the work of men of genius, men distinguished from the common herd by natural gifts. The work of genius may be imitated by men of ability and resource, or may be appreciated by a still wider group of men of culture, but art in the true meaning of creation or invention is a kind of inspiration of specially favoured souls.   Endless questions then arise as to the criterion of art.   What constitutes beauty ?   What is the relation of the artist's production to the artist's vision ?   What is the relation of art to science, to philosophy, and to religion ?   For some, art is mere imitation of nature, for others, it is insight into a mystic and supernatural realm.

Very little guidance is to be obtained from aesthetic writings.   Some of them, art criticisms and artistic appreciations, are themselves among the most beautiful of the works of art.   A great part of what is classified as art criticism is itself art and artistically beautiful in the highest degree.   The aim of these writers is to help us to discern and so appreciate the elements of beauty in recognised works of art.   Many of the most valuable have either no theory of the nature of the aesthetic fact,—they simply accept it and discourse on it as on something sufficiently familiar,—or else they conceal an intellectually poor concept beneath a clothing of beautiful imagery.   In any case their value is wholly artistic and not philosophical.   They give us no aid in the formation of aesthetic theory.   The writer, for example, who is best known, and who had the widest influence in his time in forming the aesthetic ideal in our country, is John Ruskin.   For him, beauty in nature and in art is the object of an emotion religious in its fervour.   In the historical portion of the Aesthetic, Croce, in criticising Ruskin's theory, tells us that he feels some embarrassment in including in the history of a science one whose whole character is the reverse of scientific.   " Impressionable, excitable, over-flowing, rich in emotion,—an artist's temperament—he gave dogmatic tone and an apparent form of scientific theory to his dreams and caprices in eloquent and enthusiastic words. With his glowing pages before us, a summarised and prosaic exposition of his aesthetic theory seems irreverent, for it has to lay bare his thought in its poverty and incoherence. It is enough to say that, guided by a finalist and mystic intuition of nature, he considered beauty the revelation of the divine meaning, the mark 'which God stamps on his works, even on the meanest of his works.' The faculty which perceives the beautiful is for him neither the intellect nor sense, but a particular emotion, named by him the imaginative faculty. The natural beauty which is revealed in the contemplation with pure heart of some object untouched and unaltered by the hand of man is affirmed therefore to be much higher than the artist's works. Ruskin was too direct an analyser to have meant the complicated psychological aesthetic process which went on in his mind, when by force of contemplation he fell into the artist's ecstasy before some humble scene and natural object, a bird's nest or a mountain rivulet " (*Estetica*, p. 447).

Ruskin may well stand as the type of a class of writers on aesthetic of whom many and famous examples belong to our own country and literature. They are artists who criticise art. They are deeply interested in the philosophy of art, and often give us profound insight into it, but their main direction is not towards a philosophy of art indifferent to any particular productions ; it is towards art itself and its appreciation. We go to them, for example, to enhance our enjoyment of the work of Polycleitus or Michelangelo, of Dante or of Beethoven. We do not go to them as we go to Kant or to Schopenhauer or to Schelling or to Hegel, whose aesthetic appreciation may be no whit above the vulgar, for a theory of art itself.

There are besides these a whole literature of technical treatises on art, some written by artists to give instruction on the special technique of the individual arts, others written for the purpose of giving scientific form to literary production. Each of the arts has its own medium of expression and its limitations due to the medium. None of this, valuable and essential as much of it is in regard to the practice of art, can afford any guidance to us in determining the nature of the aesthetic activity itself, and its place in the life of mind. We may set the considerations of all treatises of this kind aside as outside the purpose of our inquiry.

There is, however, a certain psychology of art which claims to be true science, and endeavours to lay down by empirical observation, and often by laboratory experiments, the objective conditions of aesthetic pleasure and the scientific laws of beauty. By some psychologists this has been exalted into a science of aesthetic, but it is impossible in this way to arrive at the aesthetic activity itself. The failure of psychology is not due to a vice of observation, but to the simple fact that the aesthetic activity is presupposed in the work of psychology itself. "Empirical psychology is an abbreviated description and classification of the infinite facts of mind ; in regard to which it proceeds very much as zoology proceeds in regard to the infinite varieties of living animals. When it treats, for example, one of the passions, love, it describes the most common forms of it, distinguishes those which are fundamental from those which are secondary, takes note of the exceptional or rare forms, and so on." "The artist has no need of any such scheme as psychology constructs ; he reaches directly the human reality from which those schemes have been drawn by abstractions. When a man falls in love he seeks no counsel from the psychology of love, but falls in love simply and in his own way, so likewise the artist does not make his works by getting up generic descriptions, he presents the lovers in their vanishing individuality." "Psychology is like the index of the book of which art is the content. The index must be brought into agreement with the book, of which it will always be an imperfect representation, not the book into agreement with the index" (*Problemi di Estetica*, p. 66).

If we set aside then the works of the great art critics and the technical and scientific treatises of artists and craftsmen, we are left with the works of philosophers. Philosophy alone can throw light on the aesthetic problem. The most famous treatise on aesthetic in philosophy is the work I have already noticed, Kant's *Critique of Judgment*. It has had more influence than any other book of modern philosophy in directing philosophical thought on this problem. Though by no means the first of modern treatises on Aesthetic, and though itself drawing largely on famous works which preceded it, such as that of Baumgarten, it may yet be regarded as the starting-point of modern aesthetic theory.

Aesthetic theory is an inseparable part of philosophy, and all philosophers in ancient and modern times have had to find place for it, but the form which Kant gave to it determined the direction of it for those who have succeeded him, and it is for this reason that the *Critique of Judgment* is important. What it has seemed to fix definitely is the place of art as the highest, or at least among the highest, of the expressions of human activity. There clung to Kant's concept of artistic and natural beauty something mystical and also something agnostical, but this mystic and agnostic character of beauty is not the limiting concept of the thing-in-itself before sense and thought clothe it with form, it is rather a reaching out towards, or a suggestion of, a higher reality beyond the attainment of thought. It disappears in the great work of Hegel, but Hegel follows Kant in placing art in the highest sphere, the sphere of Absolute Mind. Art, religion, and philosophy are in Hegel's system the supreme triad. And amidst all the variety of aesthetic theory both before and after Kant there has been a general agreement that art and the aesthetic activity occupy an exalted place above the theoretical and practical spheres of mental life. In Croce's view it is this assignment of a supreme place to what is the simplest and most elementary activity of the mind that has hidden the true nature of art from philosophers and caused endless confusion and conflict in aesthetic theory.

" In the attempts to determine the place of art, we have until now looked for this place at the highest grade of the theoretical mind, above philosophy, or at least in the circle of philosophy. But if until now we have obtained no satisfactory result, may it not be just because of our obstinacy in looking too high ? Why not make a new attempt, beginning at the beginning, and instead of laying down the hypothesis that art is, if not the highest, one of the highest grades of the theoretical mind, make the inverse and opposite hypothesis, that it is one of the lower grades, even the lowest of all ? Are such adjectives, lower and lowest, perchance, irreconcilable with the dignity and refulgent beauty of art ? But low, weak, simple, elementary are terms which in the philosophy of mind have value only as a scientific terminology. The forms of the mind are all necessary, and the higher is higher only because there is a lower, and the lower is only of less or of greater worth than the higher in the same sense in which the first step of a ladder is of less or of greater worth than the one above " (*Problemi di Estetica*, p. 13).

Every man is by his nature an artist and a philosopher, but he is only a philosopher by reason of the fact that he already is an artist. Man by his nature understands the world and changes it, but it is only because he can understand it that he can change it. Man's will depends upon man's knowledge, but man's knowledge is not simple, it consists of two forms or modes ; by imagination he gives shape to single things, by thought he relates images in universal concepts. There can be no thought unless there be first imagination. Imagination is an aesthetic activity in virtue of which man is an artist, thought is a logical activity in virtue of which man is a philosopher. This in effect is Croce's doctrine of the aesthetic activity.

Art is the most immediate form of knowledge. It apprehends activity not passivity, the internal not the external, mind not matter. It never comes into contact with a twofold order of real things. It apprehends the living palpitating reality, ignorant that it is apprehending and therefore in the literal sense not apprehending. No intellectual abstractions disturb it. It cannot fall into falsehood, but also it cannot know that it cannot. Being the first and the simplest form of knowledge it is on this very account unable to give complete satisfaction to the cognitive need of man, and cannot therefore form the ultimate end of the theoretic mind.

There are two characters distinctive of the artist's view or of artistic apprehension. One is that it is intuitive, it takes things in their simplicity, and just as they are. The other is that it is lyrical, it springs forth from within and gives expression to what is internal, not external. These two characters in Croce's theory distinguish the first ingenuous act of mind.

The application of such a theory to actual experience is met at the outset by a formidable difficulty. It is crossed by a natural prejudice, very difficult to eradicate, being in fact bound up with the metaphysical problem itself. It is the prejudice which draws the mind by a bias which seems inherent in its nature to metaphysical dualism. If we start by accepting the dualism of mind and nature, we shall of necessity reject this aesthetical theory. On the other hand, in accepting the theory we thereby of necessity reject the dualism. But herein lies the difficulty in the application. If art is intuition, then, we ask, is the intuition of a physical object belonging to external nature art? When I open my eyes and look on the first object which stands before me, a table or chair, a mountain or a river, do I in so doing perform an aesthetic act? If the answer be Yes, then wherein lies the lyrical character of this act? If the answer be No, then wherein lies the intuitive character? Both these characters are declared to be equally necessary to and identical with the first cognitive act. The answer is that the perception of a physical object in so far as we perceive it to be such is most certainly not an artistic fact, but the reason it is not is just precisely because it is not a pure intuition. It is a perceptive judgment. It supposes the application of an abstract concept, namely, that of physics or external nature. Reflexion and perception have advanced beyond pure intuition. There is one condition and one only on which the perception of a physical object would be a pure intuition, and that condition is that physical or external nature should be a metaphysical reality, a truly real reality, and not a construction or an abstraction of the intellect. In such case man in his first theoretical moment would intuite equally himself and the physical world, mind and nature, and this in effect is the dualistic hypothesis. The only objection to this metaphysical dualism is that it cannot give us a successful philosophy. Also we shall find that it cannot give us a coherent aesthetic. To accept it is to give up hope of either.

This aesthetic theory involves two propositions, each of which may be challenged and neither of which is universally, nor even generally, accepted by philosophy. The first is that there is an aesthetic activity distinct in its nature, different in its mode of working, from the intellectual activity. The second is that this special mode of activity is the first grade of the mental life, and that on which all others depend.

The best way in which I can present the meaning and ground of this first proposition is by considering what is involved in the most ordinary and elementary process of thinking. In thinking we abstract, compare, classify, unite, relate, and reconstruct the matter of perception, internal and external. But this activity of thinking assumes that there already is in existence some matter to deal with, for thinking does not create its matter nor form it. What is this matter? Some, no doubt, are content to say it is physical reality, meaning thereby that it is non-mental matter, extraneous to the mind, and wholly independent of any mental activity. But physical reality is a concept, and not a simple concept but a very complex concept, only reached by a long process of intellectual work, all which must be ruled out if we would arrive at the matter itself on which the intellect moulds its concepts. Some will say it is the mind's perception itself, but neither is perception simple nor is it free from intellectual process, for perception involves judgment and therefore logical activity. This is not the place to discuss the nature of perception, but clearly it cannot be the pure matter upon which intellect works. Some will say, finally, it is sensation, mere unformed sense-matter, a chaos, but presenting to the mind a material on which the mind can impose order. But, then, in this case the first activity of the mind will not be concept-forming, for that involves abstraction and comparison and classification. There can be no abstraction of what has no form. We are compelled, therefore, to admit that there is an activity before logical process can begin—an activity which converts the chaos of sense into the images on which the intellect can work. But it will perhaps be said this first work of the mind is not prior to nor distinct from the work of intelligence, which is contemplative and interpretative only, not creative. Yet the logical activity which abstracts and forms concepts is clearly distinct from the activity which forms images, which presents to the mind the reality on which it works. This image-forming activity, again, is distinct because the abstractions and concepts are not the breaking-up of presentations into their original sensible material, but the arranging of them in an entirely new order. This image-forming, this presentation of reality, is the work of the aesthetic activity. It is the artistic faculty. It gives us single individual images, or images of single individual things, and these precede the universal concepts of philosophy. This, then, is the ground of the first proposition that the aesthetic activity is a distinct mental activity.

The second proposition follows from it. The aesthetic activity is the first activity, the first grade or degree of the mind, because without it there could be no knowledge of any kind. Also, it is not dependent on any other activity. Knowledge does not begin with sense-data, meaning by this term mere unformed material of sensation, the pure sensation is not a fact of experience but a limiting concept. We begin with images, and images are certainly not formed out of concepts. The image-producing activity is therefore the first degree of mind. A purely aesthetic experience without any logical element is theoretically conceivable, but a purely logical experience without any aesthetic element is inconceivable. This, then, is the ground of Croce's doctrine that art belongs to and is derived from the first and lowest grade of mind.

In speaking thus of art, in treating it as one and identical with the aesthetical activity of which it is the expression, and therefore as itself wholly a mental fact, it is needful to guard against a misapprehension. When we speak of works of art we are ordinarily taken to mean external objects, something not mental but physical, whose aesthetic character is regarded as something mental and subjective, detachable from them and not intrinsic to them. In Croce's view art is purely and only mental, and there is no such thing as an external work of art. What is external in the work of art, the physical thing in which we see, or to which we give, beautiful form, is itself quite extrinsic to the art or to the aesthetic quality. Art is concerned with meaning, and for the artist there exist only images which are mental realities whatever the material the artist uses may be for the physicist or chemist who weighs, counts, and measures it and is indifferent to the spiritual meaning.

Physical science, however, does not differ from aesthetical science in the fact that the object of the one is extra-mental and that of the other mental. To suppose this would be an entire misapprehension of the whole standpoint. In science there is no externality to mind. The sciences we call natural or physical, and also history, are degrees of mental activity just as are logic and aesthetic ; they are forms of the theoretical activity of the mind. They differ only in their complexity and in the order of their dependence one on another. The natural sciences, for example, are more complex than history for they presuppose history. They are based on facts which are historical, but they conceive the nature of things as far wider than the mere actualities of events, they conceive this nature as real possibilities. These possibilities suppose a work of the mind, a work of abstraction and schematisation exercised on the simple historical events. But history also is less complex than the natural sciences and itself presupposes the world of images and of pure philosophical concepts or categories, for historical propositions and judgments depend on the synthesis of the images and the concept. We may see then that both natural science and history depend upon, and are only more complex than, the pure philosophical sciences, logic and aesthetic. It is only in this sense that the sciences of the pure concept and the pure image are inferior, that is, a lower degree of reality than the sciences of the more complex objects which depend upon them.

The aesthetic activity, then, the activity which gives us the artistic aspect of reality, which presents reality to us 'as a single, immediate, individual thing, free as yet from every logical or conceptual element, is a faculty of imagination. We imagine reality and we think reality,

and thinking depends upon imagination. Here, however, the philosopher has to meet a difficulty in regard to
the term imagination. He would indicate a faculty of the
mind and a form of activity which is not generally
recognised, and the reason it is not generally recognised
is not that it is obscure and hidden, a rarely exercised
faculty, but, on the contrary, that it is so universal, so
elementary, and so fundamental in the life of the mind
that it is taken for granted and is as unnoticed as the air
we breathe. But when we call it imagination we use a
term which, however well it may indicate its nature as
an image-producing activity, has an ordinary application
widely different from its philosophical intension. The
aesthetic activity is an actual creative activity, it gives
expression to the pure intuitions of the mind, and this
expression is the image.

It is in this original meaning of the term imagination,
indicating an activity which invents, creates, produces
images, that we may say that "art is ruled uniquely
by imagination. Images are its only wealth. It does
not classify objects, does not pronounce them real or
imaginary, does not qualify them, does not define them ;
it feels and presents them—nothing more. In so far,
therefore, as it is not abstract knowledge but concrete,
and so far as it apprehends reality without alterations
and classifications, art is intuition ; and in so far as it
perceives reality in its immediacy, not yet mediated
and explained by the concept, we must call it pure
intuition."

" In being thus simple, naked, and poor lies the force
of art. Force (as not seldom happens in life) is given to
it by its very weakness. Hence its fascination. If, to
take the imaginative illustration which philosophers often
resort to, we think of man at the first moment of his

unfolding theoretic life, his mind as yet unencumbered by any abstraction or any reflexion, in that first moment, purely intuitive, he can but be a poet. He contemplates the world with ingenuous and wondering gaze, and in that contemplation all is dispersed and lost. Art, which creates the first presentations and inaugurates the life of knowledge, also continually keeps fresh in our mind the aspects of things which thought has submitted to reflexion and the intellect to abstraction, and so for ever is making us become poets again. Without it, thinking would lack its stimulus and the very material of its mysterious and critical work. It is the root of our whole theoretic life. To be the root and not the flower or fruit is its especial function. Without root there can be neither flower nor fruit" (*Problemi de Estetica*, p. 15).

CHAPTER IV

THE PURE INTUITION

WE are all familiar with the idle mood in which we relax the mind from its attention to serious purpose and leave the imagination free. We may be watching the clouds on a summer day, the waves on the seashore, the sharp outlines against the sky in the evening dusk, and, as we contemplate the scene before us, strange and fanciful shapes weave themselves out of the fleeting forms of the natural objects. The mind is inventing or creating, not perceiving or conceiving. Its inventions are images, and these images are as different from the real objects of the world as dream palaces are different from our real homes. We are exercising a mental activity quite distinct from conceiving or from perceiving or from willing—we are image-forming. But in this case of reverie, however far we may relax attention and give play to the imagination, the imagination is never pure from an admixture of intellectual elements. The images we carve out in the clouds or waves or shadows are never new creatures. There is always in them something due to reflexion and abstraction. Memory-images of the past overflow the mind and attach themselves unconsciously and automatically to the present sense-material. No doubt it is impossible that experience should ever be otherwise ; we cannot detach ourselves from our past while continuing to be the personal, conscious individuals we are. There is therefore no actual experience of an image-forming activity, detached from the other activities of the mind. We may, however, quite easily distinguish in such experience, both at the time and afterwards by reflexion, the special activity of the mind which forms images. Nay more, we reason that such an activity must be the pre-condition of thinking, for there can be no reflecting, no abstracting, no constructing, until images are born.

Does this mean that the mind begins by forming images unsubstantial as castles in the air? The first activity of the mind, if we could experience it in its purity, would know no distinction of real and unreal, no distinction of true and false, no distinction of dreaming and waking, no distinction of thought about thing and thing thought about, and yet the world of this first activity would not be abstract but concrete. All the distinctions which make the objective reality of full experience come from the combination, the interpenetration and the organisation of all the activities of the mind, theoretical and practical. The first form of knowledge is intuitive, the later form is logical. The distinctions with which we have become so familiar that we think they are natural and original are derived from the later form—the concept.

Before I try to expound Croce's doctrine of intuition it may be well to explain, in order to avoid misunderstanding, that the terms we use in philosophy to express priority of one form of knowledge over another are never intended as a temporal but always as a logical priority. Thus, to take an example, speech is prior to grammar; speech is the condition of grammar, and grammar is the conditionate of speech. When we say, then, that speech is prior, we do not mean that there was a moment in the historical past when man first spoke, and a later moment when his speech acquired grammatical form. Nor do we mean that the infant's first babbling is speech and its maturer expression grammar. We mean that speech is distinguishable from grammar and that the two are in an inseparable relation to one another, so that, in the first moment, there may exist simple speech in which grammar is wholly implicit, a later moment in which grammar is explicit. But the inverse is not possible. There is not a first moment of grammar in which speech is implicit. When, then, we say that the intuition is prior to the concept, we do not mean that at some or at any historical period an intuition existed, and not yet a concept. We mean that the condition of there being a concept is the existence of an intuition.

"Knowledge has two forms. It is either *intuitive* knowledge or *logical* knowledge ; knowledge we acquire by imagination or knowledge we acquire by intellect ; knowledge of the individual or knowledge of the universal ; knowledge is, in short, either productive of images or productive of concepts" (*Estetica*, p. 3).

Intuitive knowledge we readily recognise in ordinary life. We think there are many things we know immediately and instinctively, many truths which require no demonstration. They are self-evident and do not depend on reasoning, just as we feel that our power to speak and write correctly does not depend on our mastery of grammatical and logical science. But there is no such ready recognition of intuitive knowledge in science and philosophy. There appears to be a natural reluctance on the part of men of science and philosophers to admit an intuitive knowledge distinct from an intellectual knowledge, and they manifest an ineradicable suspicion of it. The reason is plain. It seems to shake our confidence in the power of reason and to open the door to all the inanities and absurdities of unreason. And so it comes about that we have "a very ancient science of intellectual knowledge, Logic, a science every one admits without dispute, while hardly any one will admit a science of intuitive knowledge, Aesthetic. This is a late comer and only timidly advocated by very few. Logical knowledge has secured the lion's share. If it has spared and not devoured its weak companion, it is only to allow it to hold the humble, grudgingly yielded, post of handmaid or door-keeper. For what is intuitive knowledge without the illumination of intellectual knowledge? It is a servant without a master ; the servant, indeed, may be useful to the master, but the master is the vital necessity. Intuition is blind, the intellect lends it eyes." Such is the general position of psychologists and philosophers, and in Croce's view it is entirely mistaken. Intuition has no need of masters, leans on nothing else for support, has its own eyes, and those most trustworthy and sure. What, then, does Croce mean by intuition ? What is an intuition ?

Let us approach this inquiry as psychologists, as analysers of human experience, and try to determine precisely what is the element which Croce intends when he speaks of intuition. He gives us many instances of what he means. "The impression of moonlight portrayed by a painter," "The outline of a landscape sketched by a map-maker," "A musical theme," "The words of a lyrical sigh," "The ordinary words of interrogation, of command, of lament "—all these, he tells us, can be intuitions and can exist without the shadow of an intellectual reference. Of course they are woven

into the web of life, they form part of complex experience, but for the psychologist the character of pure
intuition is as recognisable as the character of the pure
concept. Indeed, logical concepts themselves may be
the subject-matter of aesthetic intuition, that is to say,
concepts may cease to fulfil their function as concepts in
order to serve as elements of intuitions. The famous
speech of Polonius to his son Laertes on his departure
to France,

> And these few precepts in thy memory
> Look thou character,

is packed full of philosophical maxims, but the function
of those maxims put by the poet into the old man's
speech is not their truth or falsity as rules of conduct,
but the characterisation of him who pronounces them.
The character of Polonius, which the artist portrays by
making him utter his excellent maxims, is an intuition.
The exclamation of Sganarelle in the final scene of
Molière's *Don Juan*, "Mes gages, mes gages," is an
intuition. It is not the economic concept which artist
or spectator is concerned with, when the valet, sole
witness of the vengeance of heaven, beholds his
sacrilegious master dragged down by the stone guest
into the abyss, and can think only of the wages due to
him. We are shown the whole soul of the valet in
an intuition. Intuitions are the whole of our experience,
abstract from them, and nothing is left to sustain the
concepts which are intellectual knowledge.

It will be said, however, by many philosophers that
all this is nothing more than the common distinction
between the content and the form, or, more precisely,
between the percept and the concept. In what respect,
they will ask, does intuition differ from perception?
The reply is, that perception is the apprehension of

something as real. Knowledge of reality, that is of events as they actually happen in experience, is what we usually mean by perception. Perception is indeed intuition, but intuition is much more than perception, for no question of reality or unreality arises in the case of the pure intuition. Consciousness of reality can only be based on a comparison and distinction between real and unreal images ; such a distinction cannot exist in a first moment of consciousness, for where everything is real nothing is real. " The intuition is the un-differentiated unity of the perception of the real and of the simple image of the possible. In intuition we do not oppose ourselves as empirical beings to the external reality, but objectify without addition our impressions such as they are " (*Estetica*, p. 6).

We touch in this the very essence of the problem. Is intuition a mental activity ? Is it something the mind does, or something the mind submits to ? There are many who recognise that there is an activity of the mind in intuition, or, as they would prefer to say, in perception, but they limit it to the spatialising and temporalising of sensations. Croce holds that intuitions are not necessarily either spatial or temporal, and that in any case the activity which produces them is much more general and more fundamental. It is an activity which characterises. It gives us a knowledge of things in their concreteness and individuality. This intuitive activity of the mind is entirely free from and independent of any suggestion of intellectual activity. The intuition can stand alone.

There is, however, another side to the intuition and another relation besides that in which it stands to the concept. Below the intuition what is there ? " At its lower limit is the sensation, the unformed matter which

the mind can never grasp in itself, in so far as it is
mere matter, and which the mind can only possess with
form and in form, but the concept of which it postulates
as a limit.   Matter in abstraction is mechanism and
passivity, what the human mind submits to but does
not produce.   Without it neither knowledge nor
human activity is possible.   But this mere matter
is only what gives man his animal nature, what is
brutal and impulsive in him ; it does not give him the
mental dominion in which his human nature consists.
How often are we tormented with the effort to bring
what is working within us to clear intuition !   We
catch a glimpse of something but we cannot bring it
before the mind objectified and formed.   It is in such
moments that we perceive most clearly the profound
difference between matter and form.   They are not
indeed our own two acts, one standing in front of the
other, but one is a without which we assault and carry
off, the other is a within which strives to absorb and
make its own what is without.   The matter vanquished
and overcome by the form yields place to the concrete
form.   It is the matter, the content, which makes one
of our intuitions different from another.   The form is
constant, it is the mental activity.   The matter is
changeable, and without it the mental activity would
not throw off its abstractness and become concrete
and real activity, would not be this or that mental
content, this or that definite intuition " (*Estetica*, p. 8).

There is then something which mind postulates as a
lower limit of the intuition, and this is sensation in its
brute form, pure passivity and mechanism.   What are
we to understand precisely by this?   Croce is continually referring to it so that it is something evidently
regarded by him as essential to his doctrine.   Yet, on

the other hand, he rejects absolutely, and treats as an absurdity, the idea of any externality to mind. Further, he insists that mind is essentially activity, and in no sense passivity. On the other hand, he rejects absolutely the concept of a third form of activity, feeling, to be ranged side by side with knowing and acting, into which might be bundled, as it were, all those elements of experience which we find it difficult to class under theory and practice. Croce's words often suggest the Kantian doctrine of the thing-in-itself, and give the impression that he is affirming the existence of a chaos or absolute disorder (Kant's manifold of sense) pre-existing the work of the mind in aesthetic intuition. I think it is not improbable that the historical form of the Kantian theory of knowledge makes Croce cling to this manner of expression ; but whether this be so or not he leaves us in no doubt as to his meaning. This matter to which mind is passive is not thing-in-itself, nor is it external to mind. It is an abstraction from the concrete life of mind as it exists in intuition, and taken in its abstractness is an unreality. It is a conceptual limit ; just as the concept of passivity exists as a limit in the pure concept of activity itself, so to every mental process we must oppose a mental content. When, therefore, we deal with the lowest or first of the mental activities, aesthetic intuition, inasmuch as there is no lower activity to serve as its matter, we must posit a matter for it. The matter of the intuition does not, however, stand over against the intuition to be seized and incorporated ; its only existence is in the concrete intuition itself.

There are certain philosophical and psychological theories which seem to recognise an activity of the kind such as we are here describing as intuitive, from

which it is important to distinguish the doctrine of the
pure intuition. One is the theory of ejection. This is
a theory based partly on argument, partly on psychological and anthropological observation and analogy. It
is declared to be a natural characteristic of the human
mind to endow natural, material, and mechanical objects
with its own form of conscious activity. Scientific
education is, it is said, a progressive correction of this
anthropomorphising tendency. We observe that young
children and primitive races of men invariably show
this propensity to endow material objects with a mind
or soul. So, it may be held, the mental activity which
gives form to the matter of sensation is nothing but
this fanciful work. It is to be classed with the imagination which expresses itself in fable, fairy tale, and myth.
With this the theory of the intuition has nothing in
common. The intuitions we speak of are the objects
themselves which must be formed before imagination
in this special sense can get to work upon them. The
aesthetic activity, therefore, must precede this work of
the reproductive imagination.

Many, again, may see in this pure intuition only the
activity which in psychology and theory of knowledge
goes by the name of Association. The intuition will
then not be sensation itself, but the association of
sensations which is an active, not a passive power.
Here the question turns wholly on what it is that
is associated. Are the sensational elements already
conscious elements,—can they be retained and recalled
as memory - images ? In that case we must say that
association already supposes the work of intuition, the
elements must have received aesthetic form before
they can have entered into the mental life. Or is it
meant that the elements associated are unconscious

elements, which only enter consciousness in association ? In that case it may indeed be no more than the pure intuition which is intended, but to describe the activity as association is only misleading.

The real difficulty in the whole matter is that the fact which we are endeavouring to bring to clear consciousness is itself so universal, so fundamental, and so ordinary that only the trained philosopher can distinguish it and realise the importance of the distinction. The intuition is not yet intellectual, no concept is woven round it, and, at the same time, it is not sensation but something more, something which denotes, what sensation does not, an active work of mind. There are many who recognise that all knowledge is not conceptual and that the concept presupposes another form. They name it the image, or the presentation, or the percept, or the idea (in one of the meanings of that much-abused term), but all these terms are loosely applied and not one of them by its definition excludes all conceptual and sensational elements. By the intuition we mean a mental product pure from all intellectual knowledge and a first degree of the theoretical activity of mind. It is the first thing of which we can say, Here is mind. How, then, are we to distinguish it as product of mind from the lower level of rude and animal sense ? How distinguish this first mental fact from natural fact ? Clearly not by any difference of richness or poverty of sense-matter. A character absolutely its own must belong to it. This is the character of every intuition to be expression.

" There is a sure way of distinguishing the true intuition from what is below it, a way of distinguishing the mental fact from the mechanical, passive, and natural fact. Every true intuition is at the same time expression. Whatever is not objectified in an expression is not intuition, it is not an image or presentation, but sensation and animal nature. The mind does not produce intuitions save by making them, by forming them, by expressing them. If we separate an intuition from its expression we shall never succeed in reuniting them " (*Estetica*, p. 11).

We touch in this the keynote of Croce's aesthetic theory, the theory that beauty is expression, which we shall come to deal with later. It is necessary, therefore, to be quite sure that we comprehend his meaning.

It certainly sounds a strange doctrine and must appear at first directly contrary to the plainest teaching of experience. Who does not feel that his power to express is totally inadequate to the intuitions he believes himself to possess? Who does not know the experience of thoughts too deep for words, and also of expressions inadequate to what we want to express? Moreover, how often we seem to have inspirations of truth, impressions of beauty, visions of imaginary scenes, equalling—we are certain of it—the most gorgeous visions of painters and poets, the most lucid insight of philosophers, yet nothing of this have we the power to express, lacking as we do the skill of poet, painter, musician, philosopher, as the case may be. We know, of course, that there are men of great creative genius, men like Shakespeare, Raphael, Michelangelo, Beethoven, Newton, Hegel, men who have not only had inspiration but who have also had the skill, natural or acquired, to express it ; these, we recognise, are incomparably greater than ourselves, intellectual giants, but even in them the art and the expression, the thought and the speech, seem distinct, and we imagine they might exist independently.

Natural and even self-evident as this consciousness of unexpressed and inexpressible intuitions appears to be, it is a pure illusion and one of which we may easily convince ourselves by careful observation. Indeed, we often surprise ourselves by the discovery of the vacuity and insipidity of what appeared to us, as we experienced it, to be profound intuition. The "lost chord," described in the popular ballad, is not an uncommon experience; we may be sure, however, it would have proved a sore disappointment could it have been set down in musical notation and played after we had been aroused from our reverie. How often in the state between dreaming and waking we find ourselves deceived into believing we have solved our most obstinate problems, or composed some exquisite sonnet, only to find ourselves repeating nonsense. We easily deceive ourselves, therefore, into thinking we have intuitions or presentations in consciousness which we cannot express, and the illusion is persistent. But besides this illusion, deep-seated in our conscious experience, there is yet another reason why intuition seems to us much wider than the expression. This is the fact that we give the term expression a very restricted meaning. We limit it to certain definite forms of expression, such as language, spoken and written, and the technical methods used in painting, sculpture, and music. When we say that there are no unexpressed intuitions and that intuition is expression, we intend the concept expression to embrace every kind of human manifestation. Many expressions are internal and mental only, but they are none the less expressions. Can we, for example, have the intuition of a geometrical figure, say a triangle, without mentally drawing it and presenting it to the mind as an expres-

sion ? Can we have the intuition of a syllogistic conclusion without mentally repeating the spoken words
of the propositions? Moreover, far the greater part
of every expression of an intuition is internal ; in
ordinary life the outward expression is generally the
merest sign or index of the full expression.

It is an entire illusion, then, to suppose that we
may be Raphaels, Michelangelos, Beethovens, so far
as intuitions are concerned, while confessing that we
come far short of their expressions. It is equally an
illusion to suppose that they could have their power
to express without the intuition. "The painter is a
painter because he sees what others only feel or see
through but do not see."

" Every one of us is something of a painter, something of a sculptor, something of a musician, something
of a poet ; but how little in comparison with those
who are so called just because of the higher degree
in which they possess the most common dispositions
and energy of human nature ! How little, too, a
painter possesses the intuitions of a poet or of another
painter ! Yet, however small the amount we possess,
intuitions or presentations are our whole real patrimony.
Outside them are only impressions, sensations, feelings,
impulses, emotions, or whatever other name we use to
indicate what is as yet outside the mind, unassimilated
by man, postulated only for the convenience of
exposition, but actually inexistent if existence be itself
a mental fact " (*Estetica*, p. 14).

Such, then, is Croce's doctrine of the pure intuition.
It is a mental activity, and the sure mark of it is
the expression, with which it is identical, for the
activity itself is a forming, making, expressing activity.
In regard to the intellectual function, the intuition is

independent and autonomous. In regard to the distinction between the real and the unreal or imaginary, between the dream reality and the waking reality, between the image and the percept, it is indifferent, for these distinctions are all posterior to it and empirical. The concepts of space and time are also posterior to it. "The intuition or presentation is distinguished from the sensitive flux or wave, from what we merely feel and experience, from psychical matter, as form. And this form, this taking into possession, is the expression. Intuition is expression; and it is nothing else, nothing more, and also nothing less" (*Estetica*, p. 14).

There is a character, however, of pure intuition which will make it easier to recognise than the philosophical doctrine that intuition is expression, and yet at the same time it will seem to bring it more than ever into conflict with our ordinary notions. This is its artistic character. All intuitive knowledge is artistic knowledge, all expression is artistic expression. Intuition is therefore the kind of knowledge which is called forth by the artistic nature which every man in some degree possesses by reason of his human nature. But we do not think we are artists by nature, although we think it is the nature of some men to be artists. We are accustomed to accept the truth of the saying *poeta nascitur non fit*. Croce tells us the true doctrine is *homo nascitur poeta*. Every man is born a poet, little poets some, great poets others.

There is nothing strange in the doctrine that Art is intuition. We think of artists as persons specially gifted by nature—men of genius we call them—who not only see more directly or more deeply into reality than the rest of us, but who also, besides their greater power of discernment which reveals the beauty of the world, have added to it the endowment of the skill which can create beautiful forms wherein to express that beauty. It seems to us that at least there is in the artistic intuition something more intensive than is found in the ordinary intuitions of the human mind. A difference there truly is, but it is not intensive ; it is extensive, quantitative, not qualitative. The intuition of the simplest popular love - song which expresses little or nothing more than a declaration of love, such as breaks forth at every moment from the lips of thousands of ordinary mortals, may be intensively perfect in its poor simplicity, however limited when we compare it, say, with the complex intuition of a sonnet of Shakespeare or Shelley. Philosophy has nothing to do with this extension, or extensiveness, of the artistic intuition. Philosophy is the science of qualities. It is concerned only with the nature of the artistic intuition and with quantity only in so far as it is the manifestation of quality. "The master of philosophy, in Molière's comedy, was right when he said 'whenever any one speaks he makes prose,' but there will always be scholars like the bourgeois Monsieur Jourdain who was astonished that he had been making prose for forty years without knowing it, and found it difficult to believe that when he called his servant John to bring him his clothes, he was even then making prose" (*Estetica*, p. 17).

Yet surely, some one will object, there is a complete and absolute difference, a difference in kind, between the intuition of the artist who creates a great work of art—a painting, a statue, or a poem,—and my artistic intuition as I contemplate the picture or statue standing before it, or as I read the poem. The artist has created or drawn forth from his inward soul a beautiful image and fixed it in an expression by knowing how to make use of colours, plastic material, and tones. It is *his* intuition surely, not my own, which I enjoy when I contemplate his expression.

This is not so. There is no difference between the intuition of the artist of genius and the intuition of the humblest individual who finds enjoyment in contemplating the work of genius so far as pure intuition is concerned, notwithstanding the utter incompetence the one may feel in himself to accomplish what the other has performed. It is always our own intuition we express when we are enjoying a beautiful work of art, the production of genius. The great artist enables me to express my intuition, his work assists me. I cannot, that is to say, have any intuition but my own, and it can only be my own intuition when reading Shakespeare I form the image of Hamlet or Othello, but the greatness of Shakespeare is that he enables me to rise to higher and more extensive ranges of intuition than I could hope to reach without his assistance.

" Considered from the empirical standpoint, there is indeed a most important difference between the genius who has written *Othello* and me, who read and enjoy it. But from the philosophical standpoint, the act of producing and the act of enjoying are identical, because philosophy is concerned with quality and not with quantity. The little dose of inventive imagination I possess requires the aid of Shakespeare to intensify it to the point of forming within itself the whole tragedy of Othello's passion ; and Shakespeare had no need of me or others like me to raise himself to that complex vision. I, indeed, when I read

Othello, am not identical with the artist Shakespeare, but I and the author of *Othello* are facts of the same aesthetic substance, however uneven the distribution, however different the dose in each of us, and however different the stimulation under various circumstances. In aesthetic science we do not deal with the assigning of the social grade of merit to single individuals, much less with the examination of their literary and artistic proprietary rights, we simply make our object of study the common aesthetic nature of men " (*Problemi di Estetica*, p. 469).

Croce's theory of art involves, therefore, a complete identification of intuitive knowledge with aesthetic activity. From this it must follow that all intuitive facts, even the most common and everyday facts of sense experience, are artistic facts. Consequently it must involve the denial that there is a special quality attaching to certain intuitive facts distinguishing them from ordinary sensational and emotional experience and constituting them artistic. Such a denial is of the essence of Croce's theory, and as it is the point at which that theory diverges most pronouncedly from the ordinary view, it is important to bring it out clearly.

The plainest statement of this view by Croce which I have found is in an essay on " Intuitive Knowledge and Aesthetic Activity " (*Problemi di Estetica*, p. 480), in which he replies to a direct challenge, put forward as a dilemma, by an able and not unsympathetic critic, the Italian philosopher, Professor Aliotta. The dilemma in Aliotta's words which Croce quotes is,— " Either all psychical qualities, as concrete individuals, which reveal themselves internally to consciousness, are products of aesthetic intuition ; and then sensations, emotions, and hallucinations, no less than perceptions and presentations, are artistic facts ; and this is contrary to our aesthetic experience. Or else there are some psychical qualities, to wit, emotions and hallucinations, which must be excluded ; and then since they, in the moment in which they are lived, give us immediate knowledge of themselves, or of external objects as concrete individuals, there can exist a knowledge of the individual without aesthetic intuition ; and, in that case, Croce's theory is false."

Croce in his reply elects to stand on the first horn of the dilemma and adds this elucidation of his view. " How do we get the distinction between form and matter in Aesthetic ? I have before me three different works of art, three different intuitions, *a*, *b*, *c*. Inasmuch as they are intuitions they have something in common which I call *form* ; the differential element, by which they are distinguished as *a*, *b*, *c*, I call *matter*. Now does the matter exist ? Obviously not. What exists is the form, determined as *a*, as *b*, and as *c*, three intuitions, or three concrete forms. So true is this that should I wish to express the matter of these three works of art, I cannot do so except by repeating the form of them, in which alone the matter exists. And when a philosopher speaks of matter (and he cannot avoid doing so), he means only the concept which has been fashioned by a work of abstraction and for a definite end, and which has no value except for that end. The concept, matter, may help to make clear by contrast that the essence of art is in the form ; but it does not denote an effective reality. It can indeed be presented as if it referred to something existing ; but in such case the existence affirmed is simply metaphorical, a mode of expression useful in giving plastic form to our thought. Language we know is a work of the imagination. If, in my book, there may be found some of these imaginative phrases, their value has been unequivocally settled by me beforehand by my explicit declaration that ' matter does not really exist, but is posited for the convenience of exposition.' "

This philosophical use of the term matter has of course nothing to do with the use made of it in the natural sciences and even in empirical psychology. It is indispensable for these, being the basis on which they raise their schematic constructions. They have created it for their purpose, and language preserves it for them.

Coming to the actual charge, he explains and defends the sense in which he holds sensations and emotions, as also perceptions and hallucinations, to be intuitions and therefore aesthetic facts. Is it true, then, he asks, that this theory runs counter to our aesthetic experience, or rather to the ordinary notion we entertain of the aesthetic function? " I observe in myself that in regard to any sensation whatever, if I do not abandon myself to the attractions and repulsions of feeling and impulse, if I do not let myself be distracted by reflexions and reasonings, if I persist in the intuitive attitude, I am in the same disposition as that in which I enjoy what I am accustomed to call a work of art. I *live* the sensation, but as pure contemplating mind. In ordinary life the sensation is followed by reflexions and volitions flashing past in rapid succession, followed by other sensations and reflexions and volitions. But with whatever lightning speed the succession passes it does not abolish the first instant which must be one of pure intuition. That first instant in multiplying and dilating gives place to the life of art. Without the first spark there would not be the great flame. Those who are artists in the eminent sense have the power to persist longer than other men in the moment of pure sensation or intuition, and have the power of aiding others to persist in it. Artists (as has been said imaginatively) keep the innocent and attentive look of childhood ; they are unconcerned with practical pre-occupations and undisturbed by them."

This identification of the first elementary, rudimentary form of knowledge, the intuition, and the most general and universal language of humanity, the expression, with art, explains a character of art on which Croce continually insists. Art is always and essentially lyrical. It is the outpouring of the human soul, the giving expression to what forms itself within. This enables us, too, to give precise meaning to some of those propositions about art which are generally accepted, and at the same time are found on examination to be often doubtful, obscure, and even contradictory in their actual application. For example, it is a common saying that art is the imitation of nature, a saying which is sometimes further qualified as that art is the idealisation or idealising imitation of nature. Clearly there is some truth in these sayings, but this truth can be seen to depend on the meaning of imitation. If it mean that art is a presentation or intuition of nature, a form of knowledge, the proposition is scientifically true. But if it mean that art gives us mechanical reproductions, more or less perfect duplicates of natural objects, it is evidently false. " The painted wax figures which simulate living beings and are designed to deceive us in wax-works exhibitions do not give us aesthetic intuitions. Illusion and hallucination have no part in the peaceful realm of artistic intuition. But should an artist paint a wax-works show, or should an actor on the stage burlesquely represent a wax doll, we then have anew the mental work and the artistic intuition. So, again, with photography; if there be anything artistic about it, it is only so far as it transmits, in part at least, the photographer's intuition, his point of view, the expression and situation he has endeavoured to fix. And, so far as photography fails in being art, it is just because the natural element is always more or less impossible to eliminate and subordinate. What photograph, indeed, however successful it be, so satisfies that an artist does not want to vary and retouch it, adding or taking away something?" (*Estetica*, p. 20).

There is also another well-marked character of art on which aesthetic theory throws light—the unity and indivisibility of the work of art. "Every expression is a unique expression. The activity is the fusing of the impressions into an organic whole. It is this which is always meant when it is said that the work of art must have unity, or what is the same thing, unity in diversity. The expression is the synthesis of the varieties, or of the manifold, into the one." We can divide the work of art just as we can divide the living body, but in so doing we destroy the work of art, just as in dissecting the organism into heart, brain, nerves, muscles, and so forth we are dissecting not the living body but the corpse. It may seem that the expression arises out of, and is composed of, other expressions, and not directly of impressions. We seem to have simple expressions like the "Eureka!" with which Archimedes expressed his whole joy in a discovery, and there are expressions like the regular tragedy with its development through five acts. "No," replies Croce, "the expression always arises directly out of the impressions. He who conceives a tragedy puts, so to say, a great number of impressions into a big retort. The expressions, already otherwise conceived, all come to be fused together with the new expression, in one single mass, just as we may throw together into the melting-pot shapeless bits of bronze and most choice statuettes. If we want the new statue the statuettes must be fused in the same way as the shapeless pieces. The old expressions must become impressions again, in order that they may be synthesised with the rest in a new unique expression" (*Estetica*, p. 24).

This, then, is Croce's doctrine of the pure intuition. It is the first degree of the activity of the mind, the first sign of freedom. "By elaborating impressions man frees himself from them. By objectifying them he detaches them from himself and makes himself their superior" (*ibid.*).

The pure intuition is theoretical in its character, that is, it is knowledge, not something less than knowledge, not what is sometimes thought of as pure feeling, or unformed and passive sensation, or mere emotion without definite object. As simple intuition it is distinct from intellectual knowledge which involves concepts, and from perceptual knowledge, which, though a form of it, involves what as yet the pure intuition does not—the distinction of real and unreal. It is the object of the aesthetic activity.

Let us now consider the other pure form of the theoretical activity, the logical form of knowledge, and its object, the pure concept.

CHAPTER V

THE laws of nature, which we seem to discover when we pursue scientific inquiries about the things which form our world of experience, appear to us as a different kind of reality to that of the individual things themselves. The laws of nature are truth about things, but the things themselves we think of, not as "truth about," but as actual reality. If we are challenged as to the reality of things, we reply that we perceive them ; if as to the truth of laws of nature, we give reasons. Thus we recognise in ordinary life that a certain kind of knowledge supposes an activity of mind. But besides those general principles, or those large generalisations which we dignify with the title "laws of nature," we believe that we know many truths about ordinary things which are not qualities we can directly perceive by our senses. This knowing we call understanding, and when we think about it we discover that far the larger part of our daily action depends on knowledge about things, on understanding what is never matter of actual perception, although it may appear to us equally certain. We have concepts as well as percepts, and it may often be difficult to say exactly where knowledge ceases to be perceptual and becomes conceptual.

Some philosophers hold that concepts are wholly due

to the activity of the mind, that the mind itself creates them, or rather that they are a form or mould which the mind imposes on our experience, giving it thereby the order and arrangement which subserves the necessities of action. The most famous expression of this theory is the doctrine of Kant that the understanding makes nature. He described it as the Copernican discovery in philosophy.

Without going into the argument, the fact of it and the common knowledge of it are enough to show that there is no natural prejudice of the human mind against recognising logic as an activity of the mind, such as we meet with when we affirm aesthetic to be a mental activity. Conceiving the world may be altogether an activity, but if not altogether an activity, it at least involves some activity. Perceiving the world, we naturally incline to regard as mainly passive—in its fundamental nature wholly passive—that is, a receptivity of the mind.

If we would understand the whole theoretic activity of the mind, meaning by the theoretic activity the activity which knows the world as distinct from the practical activity or the activity which changes it, we must study the pure concept as well as the pure intuition.

As we saw in the last chapter, Croce holds that the intuition is already, before any conceptual character attaches to it, mental creation. Intuitions are the matter of concepts. The question does not, therefore, arise for him whether the mind may be passive towards concepts. The difference between the intuition and the concept is not that one is a mirror of reality, the other a thought about the reality mirrored. " If knowing is not making or re-making what the mind itself has produced, are we not turning to dualism, to the thing confronting the thinker, with all the absurdities dualism involves ? " (*Problemi di Estetica*, p. 486).

"What is knowledge by concepts ? It is knowledge of the relations of things and the things are intuitions. Without intuitions concepts are not possible, just as without the matter of impressions intuition itself is not possible. This river, this lake, this brook, this glass of water, this rain, are intuitions, the concept is water, not this or that appearance or particular instance, but water in general, in whatever circumstances of place or time it is realised, the matter of infinite intuitions, but of one constant concept only " (*Estetica*, p. 27).

Logic is the science of the pure concept, just as Aesthetic is the science of the pure intuition ; in the two sciences we have the double degree of the theoretical activity of the mind. By "pure" Croce means a form of knowledge distinct in itself and free in its mode of mental activity from any admixture of other and different modes. There is a large class of general terms which ordinarily come under the designation "concepts." Any group of presentations, for instance, may be denoted by a group-name, and in that case the general term used, though named a concept, is not a pure concept, for it indicates merely the individuals composing or comprised in the group. The pure concept is through and through conceptual. Common names or general terms which simply serve in ordinary speech to indicate classes of objects are not concepts. Croce proposes to term them pseudo-concepts, and a main part of his logical argument is concerned with their nature. The affirmation of the pure concept involves the negation of the pseudo-concept.

Before I try to explain the theory let me say one

word on the terminology, it may help to throw light on the meaning. The term pseudo-concept is not a happy one, and Croce is fully aware of this ; but he is more concerned to make his meaning clear than to introduce a new and possibly more satisfactory word into the philosophical vocabulary.

" ' Conceptual fiction ' is one way of expressing what is meant, and with this there would be no quarrel, but for brevity I will use the term *pseudo-concept*, and for clearness I will call the true and proper concepts *pure concepts*. These terms seem to me fitter for their purpose than the scholastic distinction of *ideas* (pure concepts) as opposed to *logical concepts* (pseudo-concepts). On the other hand, it has to be borne in mind that pseudo-concepts, although the word concept enters into their name, are not concepts, they do not constitute a species of concepts, nor do they compete with concepts (unless we use them in that way), and pure concepts have not impure concepts opposed to them, for impure concepts are not truly concepts. Every term we can use is more or less equivocal, for the world in which these terms have to roam is full of snares, and indeed the quest for absolutely unequivocal terms is vain, and success therein would only involve the clipping the wings of human thought " (*Logica*, p. 26).

What, then, is a true and proper, *i.e.* a pure, concept ? It is a form of knowledge, or a kind of knowledge, which transcends any and every intuition which it concerns and which at the same time that it transcends all is wholly present in each. A pure concept is expressive, it is not something thought or felt but which is not spoken or otherwise expressed ; it is universal, not individual, it belongs to any one and

every one of many individuals, and is not exhausted by
any number of individuals ; it is concrete, not abstract,
that is, it is real in the full sense of the term.   What
is a pseudo-concept ?   It is a fictitious concept or a
conceptual fiction.   It is representative of a group of
presentations, it may even be of a single presentation,
and therefore it does not transcend presentation like the
pure concept, and it has no true content of its own.   It
is either not universal or not concrete, or it is neither
universal nor concrete.   Examples of pseudo-concepts
are — house, cat, rose, triangle, free movement.   " A
true and proper concept, just because it is not a
presentation, can have no single presentative element
for its content, nor can it be referred to this or that
presentation, or to this or that group of presentations ;
but on the other hand just because it is the universal
in regard to what is individual in the presentations, it
must refer at once to all individuals and also to each
individual.   Let us take as an example any concept
whatever of a universal character ; the concepts of
quality, evolution, beauty, finality, are such.   Can we
conceive that a bit of reality, given in a presentation,
however wide and inclusive it be (even if it embrace
ages on ages of history in all its complexity, and
countless aeons of cosmical life), can exhaust quality,
or evolution, or beauty, or finality so that we can
affirm an equivalence between these concepts and that
presentative content ?   Or conversely, let us examine
the minutest fragment of presentable life.   Can we
conceive that however small, however atomic it be,
there can be lacking in it quality, evolution, beauty,
and finality ?   We may of course affirm, and it
has been affirmed, that things are not quality but
pure quantity ; that they do not evolve but abide

unchangeable and immobile ; that the criterion of
beauty is the arbitrary extension of our own circum-
scribed experience and individual and actual feelings,
to the cosmical reality ; and that finality is an anthro-
pomorphic conception, laws being in reality not the
end but the cause, not teleological but mechanical and
determined.   With such disputes philosophy has ever
been and is in travail ; and I am not here presenting
them as definitely settled, nor in choosing them for
examples do I mean to determine the conceptions on
which they are founded.   What is clear is that whichever thesis concerning them prove true, they themselves
are in any case true and proper concepts, superior to
every presentative determination and embracing in themselves all presentations, or rather all possible experience;
and our concept of the concept is not altered but
confirmed by the fact that either theory in regard to
them may be held true.   Finality or mechanism,
evolution or immobility, beauty or individual pleasure,
will always be, in so far as they are concepts, affirmed
as transcending and at the same time as altogether
within the presentation.   And when, as often happens,
the two opposite concepts are affirmed in one and the
same problem, *e.g.* when finality and mechanism, or
evolution and changeless substance, are affirmed of the
one subject, it is never meant that one is to be referred
to one group of presentations, another to another, but
that both are elements and components of every reality,
in such way that every reality is in one aspect end, in
another cause, in one aspect immobile, in the other
changing " (*Logica*, p. 16).

There are therefore three marks by which we may
recognise the pure concept—expressiveness, universality,
and concreteness.   They are the characters of the

concept, but they are not separable from one another, so that one may be lacking and the concept yet be a concept. The character of the concept is to unite them indissolubly into the one character which belongs to it. The pure concept is not universal *and* concrete but concrete-universal. It is important to grasp the full significance of these characters.

Expressiveness, the first of the characters, means that the concept is in the full sense cognitive, that it belongs wholly to knowing, not to acting. The concept is the expression of the logical activity of mind or of thinking, just as the image is the expression of the aesthetic activity or of imagining. The same test applies to the concept which we saw in the last chapter applied to the intuition, the mind cannot think a concept without thereby expressing it in some form. To think logically is to speak, it may not be out loud or to others, but some expression the thought must have. If we cannot express our concept it is a sure sign that we do not yet possess it. The doctrine of the pure concept is therefore parallel with the doctrine of the pure intuition. Thoughts too deep for words are an illusion because the logical activity is that which expresses itself in concepts. A great part of Croce's philosophy consists in emphatic insistence on this point. It is indeed from it that the doctrine has received its name, the expressionist theory. Croce describes it as the *affirmation* of the intuition and the concept as the two distinct theoretical moments in the life of mind.

The character of universality belongs only to the concept, and serves, therefore, as the absolute mark which distinguishes it from any and every intuition. A concept which can be proved to be not universal is by that alone proved to be not a concept. And this

is the ground on which many of what are generally
named concepts are rejected by Croce and called pseudo-
concepts. I will quote his own examples although they
refer to controversies of his own with which many will
disagree, but the principle they illustrate we should, I
suppose, all accept. " Sociology affirms the concept of
Society, that it is in the strict sense a concept and the
principle of the science; and the critic of Sociology
proves that the concept of Society is not really universal
but individual, that it refers to such and such groupings
of human beings, groupings which have presented themselves to the Sociologist and which he has arbitrarily
isolated from other complex groupings which might
equally well have presented themselves to him. The
theory of Tragedy posits the concept of the Tragic and
deduces from it this or that necessary condition of
tragedy ; and the critic of the theory of generic kinds
of literature shows that there is not a concept of the
Tragic but an ill-defined group of artistic presentations
which have certain extrinsic resemblances between them
and therefore cannot serve as the basis of any theory.
On the other hand, to establish a universality which at
first is lacking is the glory of truly scientific thinking.
Hence it is that we hail as inventors those who bring
to light the connexions of ideas, or of groups of ideas,
or of concepts which had before been disconnected, that
is, those who universalise. So it was at one time
believed that will and action were distinct concepts ;
and it has been a progress to unify them by creating
the concept, which is truly universal, of will which is
at the same time action. So also it was thought that
the expression of language was a different thing from
the expression of art ; and it has been a progress to
universalise the expression of art by extending it to

language, or that of language by extending it to art"
(*Logica*, p. 30).

The third character of the concept is concreteness.
This, if not a distinguishing mark of the concept (for
the intuition also is concrete), is the most important
character of all. It affirms the reality or actuality of
the concept. Whatever is merely abstract is unreal.
Concreteness means that although the concept transcends
all intuitions and every intuition which it concerns, it
is also immanent in the intuition. The world of knowledge is a representative world, and therefore were the
concept not immanent in the presentations it would
be nowhere. It would be relegated to an unthinkable
world, and so would not be. In ordinary speech to
say of anything that it is an abstraction is the same as
to say that it is unreal.

The concept, therefore, is a form of knowledge
distinct from the intuition, for the intuition is always
singular and individual while the concept is universal,
and yet as real as the intuition, for it is not an abstraction from the intuition but with it constitutes the
actual world.

No less important than the doctrine of the pure
concept is that of the pseudo-concepts. The right
understanding of these fixes the status of the natural
and the mathematical sciences. It is often said that
the sciences assume their subject-matter, by which it is
meant that they accept certain representative groupings,
objects of sensible or rational intuition, as objective facts
of experience, and seek to classify them and show their
relations and the laws of their occurrence, without
concerning themselves as to any questions of the nature
of the experience for which they are objects. They
treat the different objects or classes of objects with

which they deal as if they were in themselves, and independently of any act of knowing, the real things we take them to be in our ordinary daily life. That the natural and mathematical sciences, whatever be their assumptions, and whatever criticism their methods may call for, are a human activity of prime and fundamental importance and signally successful is too obvious to need remarking. Philosophers, however, are sometimes thought to be committed at least to a rejection of scientific method. Indeed they are often charged with manifesting a positive contempt for it. Terms like that of pseudo-concept are taken as a mark of contempt, and it is necessary, therefore, to emphasise the fact that philosophy is not opposed to science but only to the claim of science, so often and in so many forms advanced, to be philosophy. The common terms with which the sciences denote the objects or groups of objects which they make the special subject of observation, investigation, classification, and arrangement are pseudo-concepts. They are not pure concepts, nor are they pure intuitions, they are simply tickets which serve the useful practical purpose of indicating certain intuitions or groups of intuitions, or certain abstract relations or groups of relations. They are " fictions " in the etymological meaning of the word, and the greater part of the dispute which has been waged in philosophy about the nature of the concept has been concerned with these conceptual fictions and the confusion of them with the pure concept.

What are the pseudo-concepts or conceptual fictions ? Are they false and arbitrary concepts to be reprobated morally, or are they mental products which contribute to the life of the mind they enjoy ? Are they evils to be got rid of, or necessary functions ?

The pure concept is, as we have seen, both transcendent and immanent in its relation to the intuition, it is ultra-representative and omni-representative. The pseudo-concepts either are not transcendent or they are not immanent. Take as examples the common terms, usually named concepts, which we have already instanced —house, cat, rose. The content of these is furnished by a group of presentations or by a single presentation, and they stand for all or any one of the group, but convey no meaning which is not given in the presentation, they are not transcendent. Take the other examples—triangle and free movement—they have no presentative content and are therefore not immanent. The answer therefore is that the pseudo-concepts both as regards their nature and their function differ from the pure concept in not being, as it is, special forms of the theoretical activity. They are useful generalisations, and they form part of the activity of mind, but of the practical, not the theoretical activity.

Let us look at our examples more closely. The terms—house, cat, rose—represent each of them a group of objects, but although the individuals in each group may be innumerable and their varieties indeterminable, there is nothing indicated by the common name which reveals a nature over and above the presentative character of each of the objects. They are terms whose purpose is to enable us to classify objects or parts of objects, and the means by which the term is made to serve this purpose is either the choice of some particular presentation as representative of all the others or the formation of a generalised image of all the different objects we class together. In either case the connotation of the term is wholly presentative and the chosen presentation is a symbol which stands for a group or class of presentations

actual or possible.   In the other two examples—triangle
and free movement—we have the converse.   They do
not denote a group of presentations nor a single presentation.   There is no presentative element in them at all,
that is to say, no single presentation and no possible
group of presentations could exhaust them.   In their
case the criticism therefore is not that they lack universality but that they lack concreteness.   They have
not the immanence of the pure concept.   " It seems
that with them we leave behind the embarrassments of
sense presentations.   The triangle and free movement
are not things of which we can state the characters and
to which we can set exact limits and which have a
beginning and end in time.   As far as thought can range,
wherever reality is thinkable, the concepts of the triangle
and of free movement are valid.   The triangle is given
whenever three straight lines intersect to include a
space and form three angles, the sum of which,
however one triangle may vary from another, is equal
to that of two right angles.   It is impossible to confuse
the triangle with the square or the circle.   Free movement is a movement thought of as happening without
hindrance of any kind.   It is impossible to confuse it
with a movement to which there is any kind of obstacle.
So far good ; but then, these conceptual fictions in
letting fall the ballast of presentations leap upward into
an airless zone where nothing lives ; or, dropping
metaphor, they gain universality in losing reality.
There is no such thing as a geometrical triangle in
reality, because in reality there are no straight lines, no
rectangles and sums of rectangles and sums of angles
equal to two rectangles.   A free movement does not
exist in reality because every real movement is determined
by conditions and therefore is a movement among

obstacles. A thought with no reality as its object is not a thought, and these concepts are not concepts but conceptual fictions " (*Logica*, p. 19).

The difference therefore between the pure concept and the pseudo-concept is not that the one is true and the other false, or that the one is useful and good, the other illusory and evil, but that one is a form of knowledge and the other is not. The pseudo-concepts are justified by their utility. They answer to a practical need. They do not extend our knowledge, but they serve as aids to memory which enable us to classify and codify our knowledge. They are of two kinds, forming each a mode of the practical elaboration of knowledge. One, the mode which forms the empirical concept, has for its purpose classification ; the other, the mode which forms the abstract concept, has for its purpose enumeration and calculation. These are the two modes, the one of the natural, the other of the mathematical sciences.

Just as the works of the great artists, the poets, the painters, the musicians, are intuitions and as such identical in their nature with the poorest intuition of the humblest human being, so the discoveries of the great philosophers are concepts and as such identical with the simplest reasoning or exercise of the logical activity. There are no more striking instances of pure concepts than the great philosophical discoveries which are historical landmarks in the progress of human thought. Philosophy, in the restricted meaning of the term, that is, as a definite pursuit and a special department of human knowledge, is logic, the science of the pure concept. The logical activity like the aesthetic activity is an essential part of human nature, and every man is by nature a philosopher as he is by nature an artist. All human knowledge has this twofold form or double degree, it is intuition and it is concept. The two elements are distinct but inseparable in the mental activity, and the term which Croce uses to indicate this distinct nature is the Hegelian term " moment." The moment of intuition and the moment of conception are not in a relation of before and after, but stand to one another as the distinct elements in the unity of a synthesis. But although the concept is a constitutive moment of the theoretic activity, that is of knowledge, the concept of this nature of human knowledge is not an original possession of our human nature, and it is only late and by slow degrees and after following innumerable false routes that the human mind has won it. And there is no finality in the achievement. The concept of the concept is not a stereotyped doctrine but the result of the continuous activity of the mind in its effort to grasp significance. The most complete form of reality is history, and history can never be complete.

The best illustrations we can offer therefore of what Croce means by the pure concept is to refer to some of these great philosophical discoveries. The first of these, because it marks in truth the real birth of philosophy, is nothing less than the discovery of the concept itself by Socrates. The honour of having founded the science of logic is by universal consent accorded to Aristotle ; we still employ all his terms and accept the general order which he gave to the science ; but the really great discovery which made a science of logic possible and on which it wholly depends was the discovery of the concept, and the honour of this discovery belongs not to Aristotle but to Socrates. Aristotle attributed to himself only the fame of having reduced the theory of reasoning to a treatise. He, moreover, recognised that to

Socrates belonged that of having first drawn attention to
the nature and definition of the concept, that is, to the
principle itself of logical science, the exact form of truth.

Another of the great achievements of philosophy,
and one of the landmarks of philosophical progress in
the modern era, is, in Croce's view, Kant's discovery
of the "*a priori* synthesis." It is nothing less, he tells
us, than the principle of a new logic, rendered
necessary by the abstractness and contradictions of the
old. "The *a priori* synthesis is a unity of necessary
and contingent, of concept and intuition, of thought
and presentation, and is thus the pure concept, the
concrete universal" (*Logica*, p. 374). And closely
connected with this doctrine of Kant is Hegel's discovery of the dialectic. Croce describes this in his essay
on "What is living and what is dead in the Philosophy
of Hegel" as the discovery of a logic of philosophy. The
concept, in so far as it is concrete, includes distinctions
which in themselves are opposite and contradictory, and
is itself the universal resulting from those oppositions.
Thus to quote the well-known example, the simplest
concept of reality is becoming, which is the concrete-
universal arising out of the synthesis of the two
opposites, being and not-being.

I have chosen these particular illustrations because
they show not only Croce's own thought, but also the
historical route in philosophy which he follows. The
philosopher, however, whom Croce honours above all
others, and to whom he accords the high distinction of
having anticipated the philosophical development we
associate with Kant and Hegel, is Giambattista Vico.
In his writings Croce finds the first clear indications of
his own doctrine of the aesthetic and logical activities.
Vico, however, great though his insight into the truth

of the philosophical problem may have been, is outside the great historical movements, in a backwater, as it were, of the speculative advance. He founded no school and handed on no tradition. Croce may be said rather to have rediscovered him than to have been influenced by him, though there is no reason to doubt the reality of the influence.

It is always, however, very essential to understand the tradition to which a philosopher is attached. The tradition gives its character to his doctrine and is at the same time a source of confidence, " because man has always thought the true, and whoever is unable to discern truth in the past must doubt whether any one but himself does in the present or will in the future possess what he in proud isolation holds sure " (*Logica*, p. 423).

Croce tells us that this tradition, so far as his logic is concerned, is not that of the formal logic, but of the Hegelian logic and the Kantian Transcendental Logic, and further back still of the Greek speculative thought. " Its affinity is to the logical sections of the *Critique of Pure Reason* of Kant and the *Metaphysic* of Aristotle, not to the *Lectures on Logic* of the former nor to the *Analytics* of the latter " (*ibid.*).

The intuition and the concept then are in Croce's philosophy together the whole theoretical activity of mind. They constitute the world we know. There are no other forms of knowledge. All that is below them or outside them is either formless,—sensations, impressions, impulses, feelings, limiting concepts obtained by abstraction from the concrete image,—or else some form of the practical activity. The pure intuition and the pure concept give us respectively in their simplest form the essential characters of art and philosophy. On the subjective side they are two modes of the mental activity. We might name them imagination and intellect except that imagination generally stands for something quite different, namely, for the fancy which reproduces and recombines images and forms the fantastic shapes we call the creatures of the imagination and contrast with the reality of the perceptual world. Imagination in the sense of image-producing is the artistic activity. It is creation or invention. Intellect is the concept-producing activity, and as such is dependent on the imagination.

How then are these two activities related? Here we touch on one of the most fundamental principles of the theory. The intuition and the concept are, as we have seen, two moments in the unity of a single process. This unity is in Croce's theory a logical synthesis *a priori*. This is the doctrine of Kant which, as I have just said, Croce regards as one of the greatest, if not the greatest, of the philosophical discoveries of the modern period. I cannot give a striking example of an *a priori* synthesis which will enable any one unfamiliar with philosophical problems to grasp its meaning at once. I can only illustrate it by reference to some famous arguments.

The synthesis *a priori* means that the logical activity which relates presentations is not dependent upon the presentations in the sense of being derived from them, or of resulting from them, but on the other hand is the intellectual framework into which the presentations (in our theory intuitions) are begotten. The concept is dependent on the intuition only in the sense that without intuition the concept would be an empty abstraction and therefore unreal, and as we have already said, an unreal concept is not even a concept, it is nothing. The unity of the individual intuition with the universal concept is not therefore posterior to experience, but original, that is a condition of experience. Whatever is not conditioned by experience, but a condition of experience, is described in Logic and Theory of Knowledge as *a priori*.

Let us take as an illustration one of the concepts already instanced, the concept of evolution, and ask what is meant by saying that it is a synthesis *a priori*. It depends upon intuitions which are single and individual. Two views of its nature and origin are possible. In the first view, that generally held before Kant, these intuitions are observed facts to which the concept evolution applies, and these facts are taken to be experience in an original sense denied to the concept. This experience is then posited as the reality, and the concept is truth about the relation of these observed facts which comes to us by reflecting upon them. In this case the concept would be what is now called *a posteriori*. It was never put in this way because to the philosophers of the eighteenth century it had not occurred to question this view of experience, which then seemed so rational and obvious that the idea that there might be an alternative did not arise. This idea of the nature of experience underlies the whole of the philosophy of the great English eighteenth-century philosophers. It found its full expression, and also developed its consequence in the well-known sceptical argument of Hume concerning the concept of causality. It also underlies the philosophy widely prevalent in France at the end of the eighteenth and early part of the nineteenth century. This was the philosophy known as Ideology, founded on the work of the celebrated philosopher Condillac, who held that all

knowledge consists in, and is, a complication of simple
sensations. He produced a wonderful book on the
sensations in which he supposed a statue to become
endowed with sensibility, and he worked out an account
of what its experience must be as one sense after
another was added. It was this view of experience
which the Kantian philosophy completely changed,
and it is this entirely different view of experience
which Croce takes as the fundamental basis of his
theory. " The concept is a logical *a priori* synthesis,
and therefore a unity of subject and predicate, a unity
in distinction, and a distinction in unity, an affirmation of the concept and a judgment of the fact, philosophy and history together. In pure and actual
thinking, the two elements constitute an indivisible
organism. We cannot affirm a fact without thinking it ; we cannot think without affirming a fact. In
logical thinking, the presentation without the concept
is blind, it is a pure presentation unfurnished with
logical light, it is not the subject of a judgment ; the
concept without the presentation is void " (*Logica*,
p. 293).

Croce's theory, therefore, is that we cannot think
without universalising, and we cannot have an intuition
without thinking. Thinking is universalising what is
presented in the individual intuition. When I turn
my thought inward on to myself it is not my empirical
self I think of but my universal nature as a human
being, yet I must have this empirical self as the basis
of my thinking. " The consciousness which forms the
object of philosophical inquiry is not that of the
individual in so far as he is an individual, but the universal consciousness which is in every individual, the
basis alike of his individuality and of that of others.

It is not his empirical self within which the philosopher retires when he seeks to know himself. It was not the son of Ariston and Perictione that the philosopher Plato contemplated as himself, nor was it the poor Jew optician which Spinoza thought of as himself, it was the Plato and the Spinoza who are not so much Plato and Spinoza as man, mind, being, in its universality " (*Pratica*, p. 7).

CHAPTER VI

THE VOLITION-ACTION

THE two forms of the theoretical activity, the intuition and the concept, constitute knowing, but knowing is not the whole activity of the mind. Man not only knows, he wills and acts; he not only understands reality, he makes it. Willing and acting are the practical form of his activity, and this practical form stands to the theoretical form in the same relation as that in which the concept stands to the intuition—it is a second degree. Acting depends on knowing, and presupposes it in the sense that were there no knowing there could be no acting, yet acting is that for which knowing exists. Knowing is to acting the first degree, the first grade or step of a single complete activity of which acting is the second degree. The two forms, the theoretical and the practical, complete a circle which includes the whole of mind, or, what in Croce's philosophy is the same thing, the whole of reality. Knowing and acting exhaust the real, there are no other forms.

Here let us pause, and before we try to understand the theory of the practical activity face a problem presented by the fact that a feeling of dissatisfaction seems to accompany every idealist theory in philosophy. We may be silenced by logical argument, but we can

never rid ourselves of a sense of something wanting in
any philosophy which declares mind to be the whole
reality.   The meaning of experience, the whole outlook on life, the significance of every action we perform
seems inextricably bound up with the notion of a
dualism.   There seem to be two orders absolutely and
essentially independent of one another, impossible to
reduce to one principle.   The one we call the mind,
the other we call nature, and when the logical arguments are brought to bear on this ingrained dualism,
we may be unable to detect or even to suspect any
fallacy in the *reductio ad absurdum,* but we always react
to a dissatisfied feeling that there must be a sophism in
the argument however well concealed.   And this feeling
is not a weakness of vulgar minds untrained in philosophy, there is in it something which seems to proclaim
it the outcome of philosophy itself.

    " There are some with a complete philosophical
system before them, and the conclusion they cannot
resist, that there is no other reality than mind, and
no other philosophy than the philosophy of mind, who
are unsatisfied, and weighed down with a sense of
illusion.   Though silenced by the necessity of the
logic, they are yet unwilling to accept this and nothing
but this as reality.   It seems a poor world indeed
beyond which there is no other.   An immanent mind
seems inferior and an embarrassment when compared
with a transcendent mind, an omnipotent God outside
the world.   A reality which thought can penetrate
seems less poetical than a reality encircled with mystery,
and the indefinite and vague seem more beautiful than
the precise and the definite.   But we know that those
who feel so are spellbound by a psychological illusion.
They are as those who dream of a poetry so sublime

that every actual poem is in comparison to it mere
dross, and yet dreaming this wondrous dream they
cannot themselves succeed in composing a single verse.
These most exquisite poets are impotent, and impotent
also are the insatiable philosophers.

"Yet just because we know the genesis of this
psychological illusion we know also that there is within
it (how could there not be?) a true motive. The
infinite, inexhaustible by individual thought, is the
Reality itself which is ever creating new forms; it
is the Life which is the true mystery, not because
it is impenetrable by thought, but because thought
penetrates it, with a power equal to its own, to
the infinite. Just as any moment, however beautiful
it be, would become ugly if it were arrested, so Life
would become ugly were it to be fixed in one of its
contingent forms. And because philosophy no less than
art is conditioned by life, no particular philosophical
system can ever include within itself the whole of
philosophy. No philosophical system is final, for life
itself is never final. A philosophical system resolves
a group of historically given problems and prepares
the conditions for other problems which will take their
place, that is, for new philosophical systems. So it has
ever been, so it will ever be " (*Pratica*, p. 409).

This quotation from the conclusion of the *Philosophy
of Practice* is Croce's reflexion on the whole theory
of his philosophy, but it touches a problem which
seems to me peculiarly appropriate to direct attention
to in connexion with the practical activity. By the
practical activity we mean willing and acting as distinct
from perceiving and thinking. Perceiving and thinking
are recognised as pure forms of mind, but willing and
acting though continuous with them seem to depend

upon a lower nature, a brute nature, rooted in a reality the very contrary of mind and opposed to it. What is this nature we oppose to mind ?

The opposition between mind and nature is one which meets us in every sphere of the mental activity. It is not only in the relation of soul and body that we seem to have, on the one hand, strengthless thoughts, on the other an organisation of a matter foreign to thought, indifferent to thought, independent of thought, and whose whole source of efficiency is extrinsic to mind. In every action we perform, or can perform, the intention seems distinct from the action, the desire or volition from the performance, and it seems to us also that we can and actually do have countless thoughts, intentions, and volitions, formed and complete, which remain mere thoughts, intentions, and volitions, and that something altogether different from mind is required to give them actuality. A thousand popular maxims and proverbs express this. And this actuality seems on its side indifferent to the thought which has given it only its particular form. Thought seems to be concerned with a matter which to some extent, and by some means not easy to conceive, it can control, but this matter would be something and not nothing if mind were entirely suppressed. For Croce this view of the world is due to a psychological illusion.

We have already considered an instance of this illusion in the doctrine of intuition. It is common and almost universal to suppose we have intuitions we cannot express and perhaps may never express, yet every intuition is expression, and an inexpressible or unexpressed intuition does not exist, indeed is not an intuition. We can easily convince ourselves of this

if we will make the experiment of attempting to bring
the supposed intuition to consciousness. We had also
another instance of the illusion in regard to the concept.
It is pure illusion to suppose that we think without
speaking and that we can have thoughts or concepts
of truths which find no utterance, neither internally
to the mind nor externally in words. But in its
practical form this illusion is much more obstinate,
seems more plausible, and is strengthened by what
seems to be the plain interpretation of fact. Never-
theless it is the same persistent illusion. This will be
clear if we now consider the general theory of the
practical activity and its relation to the theoretical
activity.

"The practical form or activity is the will. The
word will is not here to be taken in the meaning
given to it in some philosophical systems in which it
is the fundamental fact of the universe, the principle
of things, the true reality ; nor yet is it to be taken in
that full intension given to it in other philosophical
systems, in which will stands for mental energy, mind
or activity in general, so that every act of the human
mind is an act of will. We use the term neither
in the metaphysical sense of the first nor in the
metaphorical sense of the second. We use it, as in
the commonly accepted meaning, to denote the activity
of the mind which is different from the mere contemplation of things and which produces not cognitions
but actions. Every action in so far as it is truly action
is voluntary. In the will to do is also included, in
its scientific use, what is commonly called not-doing ;
that is to say, the will to resist. The Promethean will
is also an action.

"With the theoretical form man understands things,

with the practical form he comes to change them. With the first he appropriates the universe, with the second he creates it. But the second form is grounded on the first, and there is repeated between the two, on a higher scale, the relation of twofold degree which we have already found between the aesthetical and the logical activity. A knowing, independent of willing, is (at least in a certain sense) thinkable. A will independent of knowing is unthinkable. The blind will is not will ; the true will has eyes " (*Estetica*, pp. 55, 56).

Every volition is an action, and every action a volition, just as in the theoretical sphere every intuition is an expression and every expression an intuition. Whatever is not action is mere movement, mere material modification, and this is an abstraction from the concrete reality, which is action, and action is a mental reality. Volition and action are altogether one ; neither volition without action nor action without volition is conceivable. But this unity, volition-action, as well as the unity, intuition-expression, is generally thought of as a particular instance of a more general relation which includes them, that, namely, of mind and nature. The relation between mind and nature is not a relation between two different modes of elaborating one single reality, the reality of mind ; it is not indeed in the true meaning a relation. Nor yet are the two different modes two co-ordinated modes of knowledge ; this would only lead back again to a duplicity of objects. The first is cognitive elaboration, that of the true science, philosophy, in which the reality is revealed as activity and mentality, and the other is an abstract elaboration without cognitive character, for practical convenience. The mental act, the volition, has not therefore in this view another reality facing it to which it must join itself or with which it must combine in order to become concrete, it is itself the full reality. What from the naturalistic point of view is called matter is already included in the mental volitional act. " The volition is not followed by movements of the legs and arms, these movements are themselves the volition. For the physicist the movements are material and extrinsic, for the philosopher they are mental, intrinsic and extrinsic as well, or rather neither intrinsic nor extrinsic, for these represent an arbitrary scission. Just as poetry lives entirely in the words of the poem, a picture entirely in the colours on the canvas, so the volition lives in the action ; not because the one stands within the other as in an involucre, but because the one is the other and without the other would be mutilated and inconceivable " (*Pratica*, p. 52).

Apart from metaphysical theory, dualistic or monistic, this is borne out by an examination of the facts of consciousness. " Not one single volitional fact can be indicated which is not also what we call a physical movement. Volitional acts which, according to some philosophers, are consumed internally within the will itself, and thereby distinguished from other volitional acts which are translated into external facts, are chimerical. Every volition, however small it be, is already putting the organism in movement and producing so-called external effects. The purpose is already a carrying into effect, a beginning of the combat. Even simple desire is not without effects, if it be possible to be, as we say, swallowed up in desires. On the other hand, it is impossible to bring forward any instances of actions without volitions.

Instinctive acts, and habits become instinctive, are adduced, but even these require volition to put them in motion, not, it may be, in the particular movements one by one, but as a whole, just as one hand may set going the most complicated machine which a thousand hands were required to construct. Neither, then, is volition ever without action, nor action without volition, as intuition is never without expression, nor expression without intuition " (*Pratica*, p. 53).

There is, however, a very important distinction to take note of, because it is a particular source of confusion and bears especially on the concept of nature and mind. This is the distinction between the volition-action and the event. The volition-action is single and belongs to the individual ; the event is, so to speak, with God. The event does not and cannot coincide with the particular action, it depends on it only in part, in so far as individual actions are necessary constituents of the whole, but the event is the issue and outcome not of any particular action but of the whole of actions. When, therefore, we think of a particular event as single and individual, it is in truth a togetherness or resultant of a whole of varied actions. It is from the contrast between event and action that the idea of nature as something independent jof and overriding all particular actions, and the volitions which coincide with them, arises. While it is impossible, therefore, to give any meaning whatever to a reality standing over against mind, there is a reality which stands over against individual action in all its forms, theoretical and practical. This reality is the whole, which is not constituted of the mere sum total of individual actions, but is the resultant or issue of constituent individual actions. In its complete form it stands before the mind as history. There in history stands unalterable fact. It is made and cannot be unmade, but we have made it and it is making us.

The concrete reality which receives its fullest form in history is complete only in the formal meaning of completion. It is the union of knowledge and action in the issue or event. Materially it never is and never can be complete. Reality, therefore, is the living process, the life itself which is ever knowing and acting, which is never for one instant arrested, but which ever with the issue of every volition-action emerges with new form and is creating new form. In this way the whole distinction between mind and nature is seen of necessity to fall within the one single reality, mind. All these distinctions, therefore, which have exercised philosophy to determine their relations, —thought and things, subject and object, intellect and will,—fall within this reality, mind. These distinctions have been the source of all the problems which have arisen in modern philosophy.

One of these problems it is of especial importance to understand before we pass to Croce's doctrine of the forms of the practical activity. This is the problem of the primacy of knowing or acting. Is the intellect the original form of activity and does the will depend upon it, or is will, that is, a blind unconscious striving, first in order of existence? Each thesis has not only been defended but has formed the principle of interpretation for rival philosophical systems. On the one hand, the exclusive priority of the theoretical activity, thinking, has been affirmed, and on the other hand, with equal confidence, the exclusive priority of the practical activity, of willing over thinking.

" The champions of the opposing theses find themselves engaged in so desperate a struggle with reality
that in order to come forth from the conflict without
too much dishonour, they are constrained in the end to
call to their aid a third term which is then by turns either
a thought which is not thought, or a will which is not
will, or a hybrid and confused somewhat, containing in
itself both thought and will, without being either one
or the other, or even the unity of the duality. By the
one side is postulated a Logos, a Thought in itself (by
which is not meant what can think or be thought), and
it is made to adopt the resolution (how, we cannot know)
to issue from itself, creating a nature in order to be able
finally by means of this alienation to reflect on itself
and be outside itself, that is, in the grade of thinking
and willing. The defect of this artificial construction
is obvious, or perhaps we should rather say the religious
and mythological origin of it, in the comparison adopted
by Hegel the exponent of it, viz. that the Logos is God
before the creation of the world—a God, therefore, who
in fact is unreal and absurd. On the other hand, we
meet with equal difficulty in the Thought which does
not think because it has not first willed, the excogitation
of a blind will (Schelling, Schopenhauer) which does not
will because it has not first thought and which all at
once fashions for itself the instrument of knowledge in
order to be able to overcome itself in this alienation
from itself, using the freedom of the will it has obtained
in the contemplation of the ideas and in the practice of
asceticism " (*Pratica*, p. 202).

The solution of this problem in Croce's doctrine lies
in the acceptance and full application of the principle of
Kant's great discovery, the synthesis *a priori*. " In the
beginning was neither the Word nor the Act, but the

Word of the Act and the Act of the Word." Thought and volition are not parallel activities which correspond point for point, they are the semicircles which form the circle, and to discuss the primacy of one over the other is as though we should discuss the primacy of one portion of the arc over the other in the formation of the circle where the only meaning of either is the circle which together they form. There is no need of a mediating third term between thought and action, such as feeling is sometimes said to be. There is no third form.

"When man has attained the summit of knowledge (this summit is not Art, still less is it Philosophy, but History, the actuality of philosophy, the knowledge of the concrete reality), when man has penetrated thoroughly the factual situation, may he then stop and say *hic manebimus optime*, here it were best to abide? Can he stop the quivering life which clamours to be continued? If for one moment he succeed in thought in suspending it, is it for any other reason than its continuance that he has suspended it in thought? Knowledge is not the end of life but its instrument. A knowledge which did not serve life would be superfluous and, like every superfluity, scrapped. Conversely, when man has willed and is immersed in action, when he has produced, so to speak, another bit of life, can he continue blindly in that production for ever? Would not blindness impede the production itself? He must then leap from life to knowledge if he would fix in its turn the product he has lived and overcome it by thought, to which now life is the means and instrument. Knowledge serves life and life serves knowledge. The contemplative life, if it is not to become idle stupidity, must complete itself in the active, and the active life, if it is not to become irrational and sterile tumult, must complete itself in the contemplative. Reality in particularising these attitudes has fashioned men of thought and men of action, or rather, men in whom thought, and men in whom action, predominates. Neither is superior to the other for they are co-operators one with another" (*Pratica*, p. 207).

Let us now turn from this general consideration of the relation of acting to knowing to the consideration of the particular doctrine of the practical activity, the will and its special forms. The most cursory reflexion on our practical activity reveals to us that just as our knowledge is of two kinds, knowledge of particular things and knowledge of concepts or the relations of things, so, too, our willing is of two kinds, we will particular individual ends and we will universal ends ; ends, that is to say, which transcend any and every individual interest. This diverse nature of the end of our volition-actions has given rise to the great problems of ethics, problems which seem to reveal something like paradox in the very concept of morality. The solution attempted by ethical philosophers has, throughout the history of philosophy, ancient and modern, been directed towards a revelation, a bringing to light of some principle of unity between what seem to be directly opposite and contradictory tendencies. In some way, it has seemed, it must be possible to reconcile what appear as conflicting spiritual forces, pleasure and duty, egoism and altruism, self-love and self-sacrifice, for these puzzling contradictions are facts of life. Yet the only reconciliation which has seemed possible has been one which reduces the conflicting ends to forms of one another. Duty must somehow be enlightened self-interest, happiness the sum total, or at least the clear balance, of the quantitative calculus of individual enjoy-

ments. In England the prevailing tendency of our great
philosophers of the historical development has been to
reduce morality to utility. The inherent difficulties of
the utilitarian theories have often been exposed, but all
attempts to transcend them have met with scant success,
and in most cases those who have tried to found morality
on a non-utilitarian principle have been driven to find
refuge in the Ideas of the Practical Reason, particularly
in the Ideas of God and Immortality, and so in effect
have returned and made full surrender to the principle
of utility. The solution which Croce offers of this
problem of the will is precisely parallel to that which he
offers of the similar problem in the sphere of theory.
There are two forms of conduct as there are two forms
of knowledge; one is the form of individual action, the
other the form of universal action. They are not
opposite ; they are not mutually exclusive ; they are not
contradictions in the sense that to assert one is to deny
the other ; but they are distinct. Each is a moment in
the development of volition-action, which is the concrete
reality. They stand to one another, therefore, as a first
to a second degree, and their relation to one another is
that the second, though distinct from the first, depends
upon it as the condition apart from which it cannot
exist, while the first, though complete in itself and
independent so far as its existence is concerned, is yet
the condition of the second which exists from the
beginning. The individual end is utility ; the universal,
goodness. There is no good action which does not
depend upon some utility, and there is no useful action
in which goodness is not implicit.

The practical activity, therefore, like the theoretical,
divides into two philosophical sciences—economics and
ethics. These two sciences stand to one another in the

same relation as the science of aesthetic stands to the science of logic. In presenting these sciences we have to keep continually before us the supreme guiding principle of philosophy that only the concrete is real. Philosophical sciences are not abstract sciences like the natural and mathematical sciences. They do not separate themselves out from reality and present themselves with a completeness of their own. When, therefore, we subdivide the practical activity and describe economical conduct for an individual end as a lower form of conduct, and moral or ethical conduct for a universal end as a higher form, the terms lower and higher affirm no absolute standard, but only a relation between two moments of the unfolding or development of the one concrete activity. We cannot over-emphasise the importance of this principle, because the whole bias of our human nature draws us towards an absolute separation of the motives of action into two kinds, and into a valuation of these as the one base, the other noble.

"In affirming this subdistinction of the two forms of the practical or willing mind, the one utilitarian or economical, the other moral or ethical, we must dispense with the demonstration which the psychological method offers us, for this method is a vicious circle. If, however, we allow ourselves for a moment to apply this method in the field of conduct, it will at least enable us to make the two forms evident. Life, then, presents to our view, on the one hand, farmers, manufacturers, merchants, speculators, masters and servants, landlords and tenants, legislators and warriors, and, on the other hand, teachers, benefactors, disinterested and self-sacrificing persons, martyrs and heroes ; on one hand we have economical institutions — factories, mines, exchanges, banks and the like,—on the other moral institutions—schools and colleges; charitable foundations, Red Cross Committees, and the like. Have we not here a distinction as it were in our hands? Yet what the hand may touch the understanding may not grasp, and even from the hand itself what it seems to hold in its grip may after a while escape. It is so in this case. The individuals who at first appear merely economic are on closer inspection found to be also moral, and those who appear as purely moral are economic also, and the same is true of institutions. The benefactor calculates and strives to gain his end with the same *cupiditas* as the labourer intent only on his wage ; and the labourer in his turn is ennobled in his pursuit of wage by the dignity which his rough work and the moral impulses which support it confer upon him. Charitable institutions are economic enterprises, and economic enterprises are subject to moral laws, so that no one can know by striking a balance where the material distinction between economic and ethical activity actually marks a limit. So here also the truth is, that we cannot set out from contingent facts and their empirically delimited classes and reach philosophical distinctions, we must start with philosophical distinctions if we would interpret the contingent facts and understand them, and also understand in what manner these empirical classes are themselves formed, because the psychological method whirls round in what in effect is a vicious circle " (*Pratica*, pp. 213-214).

There are then two different forms of volitional acts, and every one may observe them in his own actions. Economic activity is the willing and carrying out of what concerns only the actual condition in which the individual finds himself. Ethical activity is the willing and carrying out what, although it concerns the conditions of the individual, at the same time refers to something which transcends them. To the one belong individual ends, to the other universal ends. On the one is founded the judgment concerning the greater or less coherence of the action taken by itself ; on the other that concerning the greater or less coherence in regard to the universal end which transcends the individual.

Neither form is it possible to deny. The economic form is manifest even in actions which we are accustomed to regard as altogether and essentially moral. "When we seek to recognise the purely moral form of conduct we find at once that it entails the other form we wish to disregard, because our action even in its universal significance must always be something concrete and individually determined. What we carry out in any conduct is not morality in the universal, but always a definite moral volition. As Hegel remarked in another connexion we do not eat fruit in general, but cherries, plums, pears, and moreover such and such particular cherries, plums, pears. We run to some one's assistance in the particular manner and with the particular aid which we happen to find to hand in the special conditions of the accident. We render justice at a definite time and place and in the definite manner which the individual circumstances call for. Although a good action may not be uniquely our individual pleasure, such it must become, for otherwise how could we translate it into act ? Doing is having pleasure in what is done in the act of doing it. Moreover we perceive, when we examine our action closely, that it is always subject to rational law even when its moral law is suppressed in thinking of it, so that however far the end of it is detached from every tendency which transcends the individual, this never becomes wholly inert or falls a prey to caprice. We may will our mere self-gratification, follow simply our individual inclination, yet this self-gratification must be willed coherently and not left swaying between two or more volitions at the same time. And when we succeed in actually gratifying our individual craving, when, let us say, the moral consciousness being for a moment suspended in us, we strive to carry out some vendetta, and in spite of many obstacles succeed by some clever masterstroke, even when *populus non plaudat* for our own part *nos nobis plaudimus.* We remain supremely satisfied at least so long as the suspension of the moral consciousness endures, because in having done what we wished to do we taste in some small degree the voluptuousness of the gods. We continually judge what is happening in life by this economic criterion. Actions which we reprobate morally force from us cries of admiration for the cleverness with which they are carried out or for the firmness of purpose they reveal, worthy, we are accustomed to say, of a better cause" (*Pratica*, pp. 216, 217).

We recognise, therefore, and it is impossible not to recognise, this economic form in all conduct, but we are equally compelled to recognise another form, that which we name the moral or ethical. We cannot exhibit the ethical form independently, or in its purity, separate from the economic, nor give it that definite shape which belongs to the economic, for two reasons, both of which have regard to its essential character. The first reason is that the ethical form has a universal end or purpose, not an individual end, and the second is that though distinct from the economic it yet depends on it as the condition apart from which it cannot exist. In our conduct considered as a whole, that is, as the concrete reality of life, the ethical form is to the economic form a second degree, the second grade in its explicit development. The moral or ethical end of every volition-action is the universal character of it. It is therefore the human element of conduct as distinct from the purely individual element. Were this human element non-existent, every action would exhaust itself in the immediate enjoyment its accomplishment brought, and life would be a mere heterogeneity, an unconnected manifold, of ephemeral events. No human conduct is or can be such, for the very satisfaction of purely individual desire would itself bring forth dissatisfaction. "We all guide our life according to some plan and look forward to a time beyond the present moment. In place of the immediate wish followed by a different and equally immediate wish, we set before us general ends towards which we work. For example, we propose to ourselves to do certain things and abstain from others in order that we may win the lady we love, or gain a seat in Parliament, or attain literary fame. But these ends also are merely contingent, general and not universal, they cannot satisfy our longing nor quench our thirst." "Nor can we ever satisfy our longing save by knowing how to insert the eternal in the contingent, the universal in the individual, duty in desire. It is only then we acquire internal peace, which is not in the future but in the present, because in the present moment is eternity for whoever knows how to find refuge therein. Our actions will be ever new, for reality is ever presenting to us new problems; but in them if we accomplish them with uplifted soul and purity of heart, seeking therein that which exalts it above itself, we shall in every one possess the whole. Such is the character of the moral action, which contents us not as individuals but as men,— as individuals only in so far as we are men and as men only by means of individual satisfaction" (*Pratica*, p. 219).

"No single thing, no single creature, has unconditioned value. That belongs only to what is neither thing nor creature. Conditioned for each of us is the value of our individual life which we ought to guard and defend as the vehicle of the universal and be ready to throw away as something useless or pernicious when it does not serve this aim or rebels against it. But no less conditioned is the value of every being more dear to us ; and rightly did Jesus, girding himself for his divine mission, declare that he was come to part a man from wife, child, friends, and country. That separation in union and union in separation is the moral activity, individual and universal in one" (*Pratica*, p. 220).

Such is the nature of the moral activity. " Cold and methodical philosophers when they speak of it feel themselves transported to the poetic tone ; Aristotle speaks of the Justice which is something more wonderful than the Evening or the Morning Star ; and Immanuel Kant composes an apostrophe to Duty, and writes in the conclusion of the *Critique of Practical Reason* : ' Two things fill my mind with ever new and ever increasing admiration and reverence, the more deeply and longer I reflect on them : the starry vault above me and the moral law within me ! ' And, in short, all the rhetoric which has for its object virtue or the moral law is homage rendered to that which is the supreme force of life and the reality of Reality" (*Pratica*, p. 221).

These forms, then, the economic and the ethical, are in Croce's philosophy the forms of volition-actions as they exist in the life of mind. The doctrine finds its exact parallel in the theoretical activity and the two forms, individual and universal, of the intuition-expression. In the practical sphere as in the theoretical, the form which has for its object the universal end depends upon the form which has for its object the individual end.

" Life is composed of a fixed web, woven of ever varying actions, vast, small and infinitesimal. No thought is skilful enough to carve that web in pieces, and reject some as less beautiful in order that in the chosen pieces alone, cut out and disconnected, it may contemplate the web, for it will no longer exist" (*Pratica*, p. 332).

CHAPTER VII

In the practical sphere, the sphere of conduct, as in the theoretical sphere, the sphere of knowledge, there are, as we have seen, two degrees. Ethical conduct, action according to what we term the moral law, is dependent upon economic conduct which is primarily an activity of a particular and individual order. Economic activity is therefore a first degree of practice and corresponds in this respect to the aesthetic activity which is a first degree of theory. It can stand alone ; it is not conditioned by any other practical activity although as practice it is conditioned by theory. On the other hand, economic activity is the condition of the higher form of practical activity, ethical activity, in which motives are universal, not individual, and the purpose and ideal is goodness. It is not a historical but an ideal order. The economic man does not exist as a historical fact and precede in the historical order an ethical man. It is not the order of the progress from brute nature through barbarism to civilisation. It is an ideal progression. Just as knowledge can only be understood when we comprehend its ideal moments, so conduct can only be understood when we comprehend the relation in which its universal form stands to its first individual form.

The especial interest of the economic form is that in it human nature first manifests itself in its full concrete reality. We see what makes man human, what gives to man the peculiar form of his living action, what constitutes his heritage. In the theoretical activity man is artist and philosopher, expressing his individual intuitions and giving them universal form in concepts. In his economic activity man is giving value to material objects, he is shaping and fashioning the world to make it subservient to his needs, selecting from the infinite possibility of the universe what can be useful to him for the furtherance of his life and the development of his nature. To this activity belongs all which gives form to the material aspect of human life,—natural and mathematical science, social and political institutions. In ethical activity man's conduct is directed to universal ends, but this activity is only made possible for him by the economic activity on which it depends. In the theoretical sphere it was held to be of the greatest importance for philosophy to understand the autonomy of the aesthetic moment, so likewise in the practical sphere it is of first importance to understand the autonomy of the economic moment, for upon it depends the highest form of conduct. No man can truly sacrifice self for others unless he has valued self for self. No one can even conceive the universal good except in terms of the individual good.

It is in the economic activity, moreover, that we come to close quarters with that dualism which persistently dogs the efforts of the mind to reach a consistent philosophy, the dualism of nature and mind, matter and spirit.

I will try in the first place to give expression to my own view of this economic activity and will choose my

own illustration, and I will then try to show the place
it occupies in Croce's system. I will start, then, by considering the problem in its biological aspect. Man is an
animal form which has come in the course of its evolution to obtain a complete domination, or at least a
domination which is practically complete, over all other
forms of life. Other species than the human, however
well adapted to the conditions of their environment,
live subject to man's discretion and toleration. Even
forms of life far below the limit of aided vision are
within reach of man's science. And man himself,—
how has he attained this position? By intellect. It is
the intellectual mode of human mentality which has won
for man his commanding position. I will not enter
here on any question as to the evolution of intellect nor
as to its relation to the other mode of mentality we
name instinct. Nor will I deal directly with the well-
known work of Bergson on this subject in *Evolution
Créatrice*. I am only now concerned with intellect as
it is manifested in economic activity. Intellect has
enabled man to make the world conform to his nature
and minister to the needs of his life, without which he
must have submitted to the necessity of himself con-
forming to the world or perishing. It is only to intellect that the world presents itself as hostile, as something
to be overcome, and to intellect it presents also the
means of overcoming. The intellect has overcome the
world by using the matter which stands opposed to
mind, by giving it form, shaping and fashioning it to
serve as its instruments. The accomplishing of this is
the economic activity. It appears as giving new form
to already existent matter, new direction to already
existent energy. But this distinction between matter
and form loses itself when we seek to give it definition.

The economic activity embraces the whole of our life so that in defining anything we can only define it as what it is for us, and the distinction between matter and form is nowhere and never absolute but always relative to a particular need. The forms which we call natural are so only because they objectify the world to the senses, and the senses are the individual's inheritance ; and so, even as natural forms, they are not absolute but relative to a selection which has been accomplished in the past of our racial evolution. And the ultimate forms of matter which we posit for the sciences are only useful schematisations relative to our intellect. There is no passing out of mind into pure matter, the matter is only and always relative to the economic need, and its form to the mind is always determined, and formal determination is always mental, *i.e.* ideal or spiritual, work.

Our world, then, is a human world, and for a human being there is no other world. We divide the matter of it according to a definite plan which suits it to human purposes and to the form of human activity, and this human form of the whole content of the world, the form of its objectivity to the mind, applies as far as ever our mathematical and natural sciences will carry us, for they too are relative to our intellect. Thus the whole of our world becomes a range of economic value.

Let us now look at this activity at work. No better illustration could be offered to us than the great world war which is now being waged by the most civilised nations and races against one another, and which, at the time I am writing, has been going on for two and a half years. Man is striving against his fellow-man and using in the struggle every invention, every material device which he can turn to an advantage. It is common enough to lament over the horrible spectacle of the whole inventive activity of humanity turned to the accomplishment of indiscriminate slaughter and wholesale destruction ; but it is when threatened with destruction that the human economic activity is seen to perfection. In this war we are witnessing the rapid and dexterous interplay of offensive and defensive devices. The issue is not being decided by strength of muscle but by the new tools and instruments which the human mind is designing. In the course of this war the advantage has been seen to pass almost daily from the offensive to the defensive, from the defensive to the offensive, according as some new device or disposition or weapon has met and countered some other device or disposition or weapon. There is, therefore, being played before us, we ourselves being players, a struggle for existence unlike any of the struggles which we picture as marking the course of the evolution of species, a struggle of intellectual forces meeting dangers and threatenings by creating devices, thus creating economic value.

What is particularly important in this illustration is that a struggle for existence between human groups for human ideals, in which intellect is engaged, is altogether different from "the struggle for existence" which, according to the evolution theory, results in "the survival of the fittest" by "natural selection." Intellect reverses entirely the aspect of the conflict which is posited by the Darwinian theory as a condition of the law of evolution. In the latter the species is at the mercy of material conditions. It is in no real sense engaged in a struggle. It is complementary to its environment rather than confronted with its environment as by a hostile force. Its success lies in adaptation to conditions, and it gives way to a new form with higher, or at least fitter, adaptation. In intellect we meet with a direct effort to gain a mastery for a form of life in despite of material conditions to which it is not by nature adapted. Humanity, therefore, may be a chapter in the evolution of life, but human history, civilisation, culture, mental and moral progress is not merely a part of the evolution of life, for we see in it a new and special conflict. We meet with mind in the form of intellect conscious of itself as supreme over matter. This human history may have chapters full of disaster, may be destined perhaps to end tragically, but it is essentially a mental history or history of mind.

I shall be reminded, perhaps, that in this biological evolution of the intellectual mode of activity the chief factor has been the evolution of the human brain. This is material and in its complexity exceeds the animal brain probably to the full degree that the human mind excels the animal mind. This brain has developed by a continuous evolution and like other organs, the hand, the foot, the organs of speech, etc., has determined exactly the form and the range of human action. There is no intention and no need to dispute this, nor to enter on any of the problems which arise from the twofold nature of man, mind and body. When we speak of man, human nature, humanity, we mean and must mean the whole nature. A man is not a disembodied mind nor a mindless body, nor is he a body qualified or endowed with faculties of knowing and acting. Mind, as far as our experience goes, cannot think or act without the instrument of an organised bodily mechanism ; yet human activity, whether it be knowing or acting, is wholly mental, and the special mode of it is intellect. This intellect gives its form to our world. On the plane of action it presents everything, including our own bodily mechanism as useful or useless, that is as conformable to human action. This seems to me to be the fact in our human life which corresponds to the philosophical moment of economic activity.

But the human world is more than the activity of the human individual in respect of his environment, more than the utilisation of nature in human purpose. It is a relation of individuals to one another. Mankind consists of family, social, political, national, racial, relations, so that no individual life is complete in itself, nor can be conducted in such manner that the consequences of actions will concern its individual sentience only. We are male and female, children and parents, members of groups, citizens. All these relationships determine conduct, and the conduct so determined is ethical or moral.

This ethical conduct seems to be orientated in the exactly contrary direction to economic conduct. It seems, that is to say, to tend to place its satisfaction in the sentient experience of another and different individual and not in that of the agent himself, and finally to aim at perfect disinterestedness in so far as regards the enjoyment of the individual who initiates the action. Hence there arises the ethical problem. Moral conduct the more it is exalted appears the more paradoxical, and philosophy seems confronted with the hopeless task of reconciling the value of moral conduct as pure disinterestedness with the absence of any conceivable incentive to the performance of such action. If the appeal is to nature and fact, there seem to be two principles, one egoistic, the other altruistic, in perpetual conflict in all intelligently conceived action, and ethical philosophy is mainly an attempt to find a reconciliation.

To Croce this problem of conduct presents itself as essentially the problem of the relation of particular and individual volition-action to universal volition-action. Moral or ethical conduct is distinguished from economic or utilitarian conduct not by its different orientation nor by any generic difference of nature, but by its universality and concreteness. Utility and morality are both the ends of conduct, each form is distinct and also complete in itself, that is, fully concrete ; but they are not to be conceived as two juxtaposed and parallel forms, the concepts of which are simply co-ordinated ; they are a unity in distinction and the nexus which binds them is that they are two moments in one process, the one standing to the other as a first to a second degree, so that the second degree, morality, depends on the first degree, utility.

If, on the contrary, we treat utility and morality as it is usual to do, as co-ordinate concepts, two species as it were of the general concept of practical activity, the first consequence will be (and it is a consequence which has been drawn) that morality is conceivable without utility. This has given rise to the absurd idea that there are disinterested actions, that is, moral actions which, as moral, carefully avoid all commerce with utility, and preserve themselves pure from the impure contact with it. This is absurd because disinterested actions would be proud actions, or, rather, they would be arbitrary and capricious, in fact, non-actions. Every action is and must be interested, and the more deeply it is interested the better it is. What interest is stronger and more personal than that which urges the scientific inquirer in his search for truth ?

It is for that he lives. What morality requires is that the individual in all circumstances shall make his individual interest that of the universal interest. We even censure those who do not succeed in reconciling in their own souls the contradictions between the individual interests of the universal and interests which are merely individual. "Morality triumphs over interests only because it is itself the supreme interest" (*Pratica*, p. 242).

The utilitarian controversy has easily shown that there are no disinterested moral actions. The most exalted moral action, that of the hero who dies for his country, that of the saint who suffers martyrdom, has always and must have some aspect of personal utility if it be only the satisfaction it brings to the mind of the hero or saint. Every action is in the first instance a response to an individual desire, for it is always an individual who fulfils it, and the judgment of the universal value of the action is always, and of necessity, the judgment of that individual. The important fact is that the useful action may either remain merely personal or may progress to an action which is universal at the same time that it is personal, moral at the same time that it is useful, and this ethical useful action is a new spiritual category.

There is another error, subtle and more insidious in its consequences than that which supposes there can be disinterested moral actions, and which follows from conceiving utility and morality as co-ordinate classes of actions. It is that there are useful actions which are morally indifferent. It may seem that this is what Croce affirms in his doctrine that the economic activity is a distinct moment, but it is something entirely different to this that he means. There are actions which are simply economic in the meaning that we may distinguish them from moral actions as the necessary first degree on which the higher degree depends. These actions are neither moral nor immoral, they are rather non-moral, they belong to the state of innocence before the moral consciousness or knowledge of good and evil is aroused. The error is that of those who hold that a useful or economic action can remain such when the moment of morality comes, and that there can persist purely economic actions side by side with moral and immoral actions. It is the error of supposing that there are actions, innocent and non-moral, which may persist in their primitive character even when the stage of moral consciousness is reached, having their place indeed even within the moral sphere itself. This in Croce's view is the root of the error in the ethics of catholicism. Catholicism admits useful actions which are morally indifferent, and so permissible ; then, by contrast or comparison, moral actions take the aspect of being obligatory ; and to balance the permissible actions, it adds ultra-moral actions which it names meritorious or supererogatory actions, moral actions being the mean between the permissible and the meritorious. "But Morality neither grants permissions to leave undone, nor bestows rewards for overdoing, it simply orders us to do,—to do always the moral good, to carry out always the universal mandate ; in ordinary life and not only under extra-ordinary circumstances ; on the occasions presented to us every day, every hour, every minute, not only on special occasions presented, it may be, once only in the year, or decade, or the lifetime. Nothing is indifferent to utility in the economic sphere, and nothing is indifferent to morality in the ethical sphere. In the moral sphere economic actions do not persist with their pre-moral characters, but moral actions subsist alone. The economic character does indeed give the concrete form to the morality, but it is never an element which can possess a value of its own in the moral life " (*Pratica*, p. 244).

A comparison with the doctrine of the theoretical activity will serve to make Croce's criticism of the theory of permissible or morally indifferent actions clearer. Economic actions are non-moral in the same meaning in which intuitions or artistic impressions are alogical, neither true nor false. Intuitions burst forth spontaneously, but the spontaneity is continually giving place to fixity. The intuition becomes concrete in the expression, and takes its place as an intuition among intuitions, and so even in its purely intuitional state may be said to include the universal within itself. But when the philosophical moment supervenes on the artistic moment what till now were pure intuitions are changed. The world of intuitions in which reality and unreality were undistinguished is transfigured into a world of perceptions. What before were poetical images are now submitted to criticism or reflexion. They become interpenetrated with concepts, discriminated into images which exist and images which are possible. In the world of perception or of history no single poetical element can persist any longer as such. What in the pure field of art is enchanting truth, when transferred to history is discordant, is changed to repulsive falsehood. We see this illustrated in those histories in which fictions and fables are intermingled with narration of events. History itself indeed assumes artistic form, but this is the form of the history itself ; we cannot introduce art into history as an independent element. There is an exact analogy in the sphere of conduct. Utilitarian volitions are its intuitions, moral volitions are its perceptions ; the former correspond to art, the latter to history. The economic volitions are morally indifferent in so far as and to the degree that they precede the moral consciousness ; but within this consciousness they lose the right of innocence, just as the pure intuitions having become perceptions lose in history the right they enjoyed as pure intuitions. So the ethical discrimination of the economic volitions, which is accomplished by means of the moral consciousness, corresponds completely with the historical discrimination of the aesthetic intuitions, which is accomplished by means of the logical consciousness.

What leads us in ordinary life to treat utilitarian and moral actions as co-ordinates, and to present them to ourselves as contrary in their nature, two opposite species, irreconcilable, divergent in their direction, so that to pursue a purely moral end appears as the direct negation of the pursuit of a purely utilitarian end, is that in the one kind of action the immediate incentive seems to be pleasure in the meaning of sensual gratification, while in the other case pleasure is never the incentive, and if it enter into the consideration at all does so only in a derived and often metaphorical sense, never in the primitive sense. As pleasure and pain seem to be the universal incentives and deterrents of actions, not only for human actions but as far as we can judge by analogy, wherever there is consciousness, moral actions present themselves to us as a kind of non-natural action. We endeavour to reconcile the contradiction by the concept of happiness as a kind of

spiritual satisfaction which may be consistent even with
an accompaniment of actual physical pain. But try
how we will we seem unable to escape an ultimate
opposition between actions which are natural and
actions which are, in whatever way we account for
them, non-natural. Some moralists seize on this fact
as evidence that moral actions are due to what is called
the voice of conscience, and they attribute this to a
spiritual influence of a transcendent order superposed
on our brute nature, a theory which finds expression in
the Christian doctrine of the grace of God.

It is on this fundamental problem of the relation of
the natural and the moral man that Croce's doctrine of
the economic activity is most significant. He presents
to us a mode of conceiving the practical life in which
these apparently divergent tendencies are not indeed
reconciled, but shown to be in no need of reconciliation.
The nexus of useful and moral actions and their
necessary distinction in their necessary unity is not an
adjustment *a posteriori*, but a synthesis *a priori*. I will
endeavour to explain this by showing first what it is
that Croce denies and then what it is that he affirms in
this theory of the relation between the economic and
the ethical form of conduct.

What is denied is that pleasure and pain which go
by the generic name of feeling, or the feelings, constitute a special form of mind. There is no moment
in the activity of mind which we can distinguish as the
moment of feeling, autonomous and distinct from the
moment of knowing and the moment of doing. We
have already more than once had to notice the importance of this denial of a third form of mind, or
rather, we should say, of a first form of mind before
either knowing or doing and on which these activities

may be said to depend. What is of importance, however, in the present connexion is that the denial cuts
away at once the ground for a distinction between
utilitarian and ethical actions which would make the
first depend on feeling, the second on knowledge.
The usual psychological doctrine regards feeling as
the substance or substratum of experience, the passive
element upon which or from which the psychical
activity develops. The characteristic note of Croce's
philosophy is the rejection of a passive element of
experience ; mind in every form is essentially activity.
(I would refer the reader who desires to see the full
import of this doctrine and its relation to current
theory, to an article by Professor J. A. Smith, "On Feeling," in *Proceedings of the Aristotelian Society*, vol. xiv.)

What is affirmed in this doctrine of the economic
activity is that what we call feeling and describe as
pleasures and pains is in fact identical with the economic
activity itself. When we isolate feeling from ethical
action, or treat such action as uninfluenced by feeling,
what we are isolating and distinguishing is low-grade
economic action from high-grade ethical action. This
low-grade action has its moment of independent and
autonomous existence. It appears, for example, in
isolation and independence in the animals, for we think
of them as without the moral life ; and it appears,
isolated also to a certain degree and in an abstract
sense, in our own experience, whenever we think of our
primitive impulses as preceding our rational conduct.
It is clear that when feeling is thus distinguished from
the moral activity and contrasted with it the contrast is
between ethical activity and the pure economic activity
itself. This economic activity is expressed as pleasure
and pain and it is identical with its expression.

It is to be noted here that in speaking of pleasures and pains under the generic name of feeling, we intend the terms in their psychical meaning as constituents of conscious experience. We are not concerned with the physiological problem of their nature and purpose in the organism. Physiology presents an important, but for psychology and philosophy a narrowly abstract view, of them. Great light has been thrown on the nature of pain by the physiological discovery of specific nerve-endings of pain. This discovery of the physiological condition, although not irrelevant, for no aspect of the problem is irrelevant, has no direct bearing on the psychical problem of the part which pain plays in the activity of the mental life.

To return to the main argument, a far-reaching consequence follows from the identification of feeling with economic activity. This is that pleasure is the positive expression of the economic activity, pain its negation. As, then, it is the positive economic activity on which ethical activity depends, for only the positive is, and as the positive expression of ethical activity is duty, there can never really be an opposition between pleasure and duty ; the two terms must coincide. " When we speak of a good action accompanied by pain our words are a contradiction, or, rather, we are using a mode of expression which cannot be meant literally. A good action, in so far as it is good, always brings satisfaction and pleasure. If it be accompanied by pain it can only be that the good action is not yet wholly good, either because not willed with full inward accord, or else because, besides the moral action, which itself is pleasing, there is a new practical problem yet unsolved and therefore painful " (*Pratica*, p. 248). All the systems which have opposed

morality to pleasure have used the term pleasure in a
restricted sense, for to deprive the moral act of pleasure
absolutely would be to destroy it even as a moral act.
It would be like depriving thought of words and all other
forms of expression and supposing we might still think.

Croce accordingly rejects every theory which sub-
ordinates pleasure or happiness to duty or virtue,
utilitarian activity to moral activity.   From the side of
morals the subordination of the one term to the other
is impossible, for it is on the one term that the other
depends.   Within the ethical circle itself the subordination is equally impossible, for though indeed there are
two terms they are united in one, one is not above the
other.   " Morality has absolute sway over life, and
there is no act of life however mean we may think it
which morality does not or must not rule.   But morality
wields no authority over the forms and categories of
the mind ; and as it cannot destroy or modify itself,
so it cannot destroy or modify the other mental forms
which are its necessary support and presupposed by it "
(*Pratica*, p. 250).

Such is Croce's doctrine of the two forms of the
practical activity.   It is a bold and radical application
of a philosophical principle, the principle of the *a priori*
synthesis, to the ethical problem.   Radical in what it
denies, radical in what it affirms, the ethical problem
dissolves before it.   Psychical action is distinguished
from every other form of action by the fact that it is
conditioned by and depends upon knowing.   The
mark of the psychical action even in its lowest form is
the perception which precedes it.   Knowing is therefore
involved in all psychical activity.   There is no form of
mind, no feeling, deeper and more fundamental than
knowing.   What, then, is that aggressively real form of

experience we term pleasure-pain? It is the expression
of economic activity, the autonomous form of animal
utilitarian action. It is the form in which actions are
particular individual actions and, therefore, the lower
grade of action. Ethical action is the higher grade,
the universal. It depends on the lower for the
material which gives it concreteness, but when the
higher is reached the lower is not left behind but
raised to the higher degree.

CHAPTER VIII

LIFE or mind, studied as philosophy studies it, that is as concrete reality, is an activity which, as it unfolds, presents itself to our view under two.main aspects, first as an activity of knowing and second as an activity of doing or acting. Each of these activities is also subdivided. Knowing is, in the first place, a knowledge of particular images, and in the second place a knowledge of universal relations. Doing also is, in the first place, economic, actuated by individual ends, and in the second place ethical, actuated by universal ends. There are therefore four moments, using the term moment in the philosophical meaning already explained, in the unfolding of mind. These four moments stand to one another in a definite relation, they are not interchangeable. The logical or philosophical order of this development is named by Croce the twofold degree. The first moment is independent of the second moment except in so far as it conditions the second, whereas the second moment is dependent on the first, the first being the condition of it. Knowing and doing stand to one another in the same logical order. Knowing is independent of doing save in so far as it is the condition of doing, but doing is dependent on knowing as its condition. In like manner, knowing is an activity of twofold degree. Its first moment is intuition, and intuition is individual, the immediate expression, or taking shape, of the image. The second moment is the concept in which the image is universalised. So, also, doing has two moments in this same relation of twofold degree. In the first moment the end of the action appears as the immediate utility to the individual ; in the second moment, as its universal or ethical aspect. This double division of mental activity gives us four moments of full unfolding or development, the first, the intuition, being alone independent of those which succeed ; the second the concept, dependent on the first but independent of the others ; the third, the individual end or the utility dependent on both those below it but independent of the fourth ; the fourth, the ethical end, being dependent on all three below it.

These moments are not abstract, nor are they separate parts of the whole activity. We cannot take one away and still possess the rest. Each moment is fully concrete, which means that it presents the whole reality under one of its aspects. Each is therefore a pure, universal, concrete concept, and each concept is distinct. These four distinct concepts are the beautiful, the true, the useful, and the good. In the first moment of its activity all reality is presented as beauty ; in the second moment, as truth ; in the third moment, as utility ; and in the fourth moment, as goodness. Each of these—beauty, truth, utility, goodness—is a pure concept, which means, as we have already seen, that each concept is truly universal and not merely general. It is not, that is to say, a group-name for a class of particular objects, presenting some common features which it is useful to denote. Each expresses and is the

essential quality, character, or nature of the fact—
the quality which makes the fact what it is in itself,
and not some abstract quality or character arbitrarily
separated out for a scientific or any other kind of
practical purpose.   Also each is a concrete concept, it
expresses the full reality and the whole reality.   It is
not an incomplete fact waiting for another concept to
give it complete reality.   And especially each is a distinct concept.   This brings us to the doctrine which is
fundamental and characteristic in Croce's philosophy,
and will require a detailed exposition.

Let us pause, however, one moment, in order to be
prepared for an objection which is probably already on
the lips of every one who is becoming acquainted with
this doctrine for the first time.   How can a concept,
it will be said, embrace the whole reality ?   We may
indeed use a term to comprehend the universe in its
immensity and immeasurable variety, but will not
such a term come under condemnation as a pseudo-
concept ?   Is it more than a practical device by which
we denote the class of all classes ?   Can any such
concept of the whole be characteristic and qualitatively
inclusive as well as numerical and quantitatively
inclusive ?   If reality be a whole, it is a whole of
infinite diversity.   The universe, even for us, is full of
a number of things.   Some are beautiful, but only in
comparison with others which are indifferent or even
ugly and repulsive.   Some propositions are true, but
also many which have seemed true have proved false ;
and, doubtless, many which now seem true are errors.
In any case error is as patent as truth.   Some things
are useful, but most things are indifferent, and many
things are worthless or even noxious.   Some conduct
is good, but also sometimes even the best intentioned

conduct produces only evil. How, then, even if the thesis be granted that mind is reality, can any concept express the quality of the whole ?

In speaking of the whole of reality, or of reality as a whole, no philosopher, I imagine, supposes that reality is exhaustible, or that the universe is complete in the sense that the beginning and end of history can be grasped in any concept. What is meant by the whole of reality is every possible form of it. In identifying reality with mind, Croce means that there is no form of reality which is not a form of mental activity, or, as he would perhaps say, of immanent mind ; and also that philosophy can present all the forms in such a systematic and organic unity that we are able to affirm there are no others.

The theory of the distinct concept is the most important part of Croce's philosophy, the corner-stone of his system. He is indebted for it to Hegel, but he claims for it that it marks an advance on the Hegelian doctrine. It retains what is living in the philosophy of Hegel while rejecting what is dead. So far as it is a discovery in philosophy, the whole glory of that discovery belongs to Hegel, but so far as it is a development of that discovery, it reveals a truth hidden from its discoverer. Briefly, the theory is, firstly, that every concept is a unity of opposites. Opposites are to a concept as the two poles of the magnet, positive and negative, only to be defined by their relation to one another, only actual in their unity. This unity is a synthesis *a priori*, and separate from the unity the component elements are abstract and unreal. Each in abstraction is the negation of the other, but each in being posited posits the other. Secondly, the distinct concept, though a unity of opposites, is not in its turn itself an opposite. It is not a thesis to which another distinct concept offers an antithesis, the two requiring to be unified in a higher synthesis. There is no standpoint from which the distinct concept is itself an unreal abstraction. On the contrary, the distinct concept is a degree of reality. The degrees of reality are not triads as Hegel taught—thesis, antithesis, synthesis; the degrees are twofold. The first is the condition which makes the second possible. The second is higher than the first only in the sense that it depends upon it as its condition. One is not above another in dignity. This is the theory in bare outline. The clearest exposition of it is in the essay, " What is living and what is dead of the philosophy of Hegel."

This logical method was named by Hegel dialectic. In Hegel's logic we are shown each synthesis or unity of opposites, as it is reached, become in its turn the thesis of a new triad, and by an ascending series of triads thought advances to its goal, the absolute idea. Starting with the barest of the categories, *being*, the antithesis of which is *nothing*, we reach the first concrete concept *becoming*, the synthesis of being and nothing. Becoming now stands as the thesis in a new triad, and so we progress until we reach the highest triad in which Art is the thesis, opposed to Religion which is its antithesis, and the synthesis of the two opposites is Philosophy.

Croce's scheme is entirely different. In his system Art is already fully concrete ; it posits no negation. It is a first degree of reality, the first moment in the unfolding or development of the activity of mind. Philosophy is the second degree, but philosophy is not the opposite of art, it is distinct from it although without art as the condition there can be no philosophy.

And though Croce would agree with Hegel in placing philosophy higher than religion, holding that it is more universal and more concrete than religion, he does not conceive religion as the antithesis of art, nor as the antithesis of philosophy. Art and philosophy for Croce together constitute the theoretic activity, that is, they exhaust all that we mean or can mean by knowing. Knowing, also, is distinct from doing, theory from practice ; but doing is not the antithesis of knowing, practice is not the antithesis of theory. Action separated from knowledge is not action ; it is mere mechanical movement, mere nature, abstract and therefore not independently real. Practice also has two degrees, the economic and the ethical, but they do not stand in the relation thesis—antithesis. In all action the fundamental consideration is utility ; this is the first degree. The second degree is moral, its end is goodness.

This twofold relation of the degrees of reality to one another, as distinct from the Hegelian triad, is the characteristic feature of Croce's method. No distinct concept stands to another distinct concept as its antithesis or opposite. For example, intuition is not the opposite of thought, nor is thought the antithesis of intuition, nor do thought and intuition require reconciliation. Thought depends entirely and throughout on intuition, and there is no intuition which does not enter into the universalising relation of thought. Truth is distinct from beauty, goodness from usefulness, but they are not pairs of opposites. Yet each of these distinct concepts is itself a unity or synthesis of opposites. The concept of beauty is not the concept of some character which exists, or could exist, in pure abstraction from the character which is its opposite ugliness. Ugliness is an element in the concept of beauty. The two characters, the beautiful and its opposite the ugly, unmeaning and unreal and undefinable in abstraction from one another, exist only in the synthesis of the distinct concept beauty. So also truth, the distinct concept, is a synthesis of the opposites truth and error ; and the same is true of the concepts of practice, utility and goodness ; they include and do not exclude worthlessness and evil.

The problem I have been trying to expound by comparing the theory of Croce with that of Hegel, despite its dialectical form, is not in fact an abstruse problem which concerns only those who care to amuse themselves with a kind of mental gymnastic. It is a problem which intimately concerns us all. No one who lives our human life and thinks our human thoughts can cast it aside as a thing indifferent and of no importance, for it touches the fundamental principle of our existence. It lies dormant in every man's thought, repressed, it is true, for most men, by the stern necessity imposed on us of attention to life, but ever ready to awaken and spring up in the mind when the strain of action is relaxed and we turn to contemplation. It is essentially the problem which has exercised philosophy throughout its whole history, and not only the minds of those whom we name philosophers in a special sense. It is present to all who reflect. In the Greek world and to the Greek philosophers it was the problem of knowledge and opinion, the problem of wisdom. In the Christian world it has centred round the moral problem of the nature of evil.

Presented as philosophy presents it, the theory of the synthesis of opposites in a pure concept bears to the ordinary man a paradoxical character, which his common sense, impatient of speculative reasoning, is content to

cast aside as frivolous when brought into contact with
the practical reality of life.   This is especially the case
with the initial proposition of Hegel, the synthesis of
the opposites being and nothing in the concept of
becoming.   Hegel in choosing to begin the illustration
of his logical method by taking the barest category of
thought, instead of bringing immediate conviction, has
seemed to most people to have thrown down a stumbling-
block and rock of offence at the very threshold of his
undertaking.   Hegel was himself aware of this.   " No
great amount of wit," he remarks, " is needed to throw
ridicule on the maxim that Being and Nothing are
the same, or even to represent the absurdities which, it
is falsely said, are the consequences and illustrations
of that maxim " (*Logic of Hegel, Wallace's Translation*,
p. 140).   Yet even when we feel no doubt that there
may be some rational doctrine behind, in its plain and
obvious meaning the theory of the dialectic seems to us
indefensible.   Could it be defended it would, we think,
be the end not the beginning of philosophic wisdom.
It must mean in the most literal sense that all is vanity.

We may, however, understand the principle more
readily if for the bare categories, being and nothing, we
substitute a pair of more concrete opposites, such as
life and its negation death.   Life and death are two
opposed terms, each of which, taken abstractly, is the
mere negation of the other.   Death as well as life
carries for all of us a very full meaning.   Taken in
abstraction, the two ideas are incompatible.   To affirm
one is to deny the other.   Yet the distinct concept of
life, the concept of life which presents the full concrete
reality is a synthesis of these two opposites—life and
its negation death.   We cannot posit either without
bringing the other into the concept as an essential and

intimate part of the concept. Let us put it to the test. Death is a negation, but it is not pure nothingness ; were it so it would be entirely devoid of sense. On the contrary, it is for human thought a concept pregnant with meaning. We clothe it with imagery. Death is the king of terrors, the adversary, the solemn and dreaded enemy, it stalks through the land, or it is the reaper, or the longed-for solace of the wretched. Whence does this abstract pure negation, this simple absence of something, derive its substantial clothing and stand before us as a positive reality? What is the reality which is thus opposed to the reality of life ? Every attribute of death is an attribute of life, and death, in so far as we affirm it, is identical with the life which in affirming death we negate. Consider now the affirmation, life, which stands over against the negation death. Can we conceive life without conceiving its negation ? It is impossible. Its meaning can only be expressed in its contrast with what it is not. This is evident in the very language we use. The word immortality expresses the negation of the negation death. We can only present the idea of eternal life in terms of death, as when we speak of the undying gods. Yet, it will be said, whatever our mode of expression, there is in life a positive content, and in the concept of life a positive meaning which is absent from the concept of death. In so far, however, as life is a distinct concept it includes and does not exclude its opposite death, the concept is a synthesis or unity of opposites. If we break this unity and separate it into two abstract concepts, on the one hand a life which excludes death, on the other, a death which excludes life, we have got two abstract ideas. Abstractions are not and cannot be realities. This purely logical fact can be applied to our

everyday notion of life and death. Life in its fulness
is the continual, ever-renewed succession of doing and
done, of done and doing, of acting and acted, of acted
and acting—of death and life.

The principle is so important that it is worth while
to illustrate its working on a much lower plane than
that which I have taken in the example of life as a
synthesis of life and death. We may take instead a
trivial example chosen from the empirical sphere. Let
us take the pair of opposite or antithetical terms, wet
and dry. No distinct concept of wetness, or of dryness,
is possible which does not hold within it the two ideas,
the positive wet and its negation dry, or the positive
dry and its negation wet. Take either in pure
abstraction from the other, separate its notion completely from the notion of the other, and we find the
notion we seem to have is not a concept or notion
of anything at all. Our notions of wet, for example,
can never enter the experience of a fish because a
condition of the fish's life is that it should be always
what we call wet. It could never, therefore, possess
our notion of wetness simply because for it the negation
of wetness is impossible.

Every concept in so far as it is distinct is concrete.
It holds together in an original synthesis two opposite
terms, neither of which taken in pure abstraction from
the other conveys any meaning at all, or, what is the
same thing, each of which derives its meaning from
the other to which it stands opposed. One term of
these two opposites is in its first intention simply the
negation of that of which the first is the affirmation.
Such is the principle which underlies the important
philosophical doctrine named dialectic. It gives the
distinguishing character to the special method of

philosophy. Philosophy is the study of the concrete.
Croce considers that this special method or logic of
philosophy, the discovery of Hegel, marks the greatest
advance in the science in the whole of the modern era.
It was a discovery made possible and only made
possible by the other great discovery, the discovery
by Kant of the Synthesis *a priori*.

"Hegel is one of those philosophers who have made
not only immediate reality but philosophy itself an
object of their thinking, thus contributing to the
elaboration of a *logic of Philosophy*. The logic of
philosophy, moreover (with the consequences ensuing
from it for the solution of particular problems and for
the conception of life), seems to have been the goal to
which the main effort of his mind was directed. In
it he formed or brought to perfection and gave value
to, principles of high importance which had been
unknown to previous philosophers, or only hinted at
by them, and which therefore may be considered to
be his true discoveries " (*Saggio sullo Hegel*, p. 3).

" The threefold character which the philosophical
thought assumes ought to be put clearly in contrast to
the three mental modes or attitudes with which this
threefold character is usually and very easily confused.
For Hegel the philosophical thought is, firstly, a
concept, secondly, universal, and thirdly, concrete.
It is a concept, that is to say it is not feeling, or
rapture, or intuition, or any other similar alogical state,
and is not devoid of demonstrative force. It is this
character which is the distinguishing mark of philosophy
in regard to the theories of mysticism and direct
revelation ; theories which have, at the most, a negative
significance, in that they recognise that philosophy
cannot be constructed by the method of the empirical

and natural sciences, the sciences of the finite, and which if they be profound have an 'empty profundity.' Against mysticism, and the prophetic forebodings and the mysterious phrases of its initiates, the frenzies, the sighings, the raising the eyes to heaven, the bowing the neck and clasping the hands, the swooning, Hegel's satire grows fierce. He insists that philosophy must have reasoned and intelligible form ; must be 'not esoteric but exoteric,' not a thing of sects but of humanity. The philosophical concept is *universal* and not merely general. It is not to be confused with general ideas, such, for example, as 'house,' 'horse,' 'blue,' which we usually term concepts, an abuse which Hegel calls a barbarism. It is this character, universality, which marks the difference between philosophy and the empirical or natural sciences, for these are satisfied with types and concepts of classes. Finally, the philosophical universal concept is *concrete*: not a skeletonising of reality, but the comprehension of it in its fulness and richness. Philosophical abstractions are not arbitrary but necessary, they are adequate to reality, they do not either mutilate it or falsify it. And this character, concreteness, marks the difference between philosophy and the mathematical sciences ; for these sciences do not justify their starting-points, they 'demand them' ; and we have, says Hegel, to obey the demand and draw such and such lines in good faith that in so doing we shall keep step with the demonstration. Philosophy, on the contrary, has for its object what really is, and it must justify itself fully, neither admitting a presupposition nor allowing any presupposition to subsist" (p. 6).

Opposition is therefore something which holds within every distinct concept. The concept is like an organism, it is the harmony, the equilibrium, the reconciliation of constituent forces which, apart from their unity in the organism, are antagonistic and mutually destructive. It is the very fact that these oppositions, the affirmation and its negation, exist together in indissoluble unity, difference in identity, which gives to the distinct concept its concrete character, and makes it an adequate expression of reality.

" The philosophical concept inasmuch as it is concreteness, does not exclude distinctions, indeed it includes them in itself. It is the universal, distinct in itself, and resulting from those distinctions. As empirical concepts are distinguished into classes and sub-classes, so the philosophical concept has its own particular forms, but it is not the mechanical aggregate of them, it is rather the organism, in which every form is united intimately with the others and with the whole. For example, the imagination and the intellect are particular philosophical concepts in regard to the concept of mind or of mental activity ; but they are not outside mind or below mind, they are indeed mind itself in those particular forms ; nor is the one separated from the other like two entities each enclosed within itself, and external to the other, but the one passes into the other. Hence the imagination, as is commonly said, however distinct it may be from the intellect, is the foundation of the intellect and indispensable to it " (p. 8).

Any one may watch this process also who will attend closely to the working of his own mind. New experience comes to us in the form of presentation, and this is always particular and individual, the shaping of impressions into definite images of an objectified reality. This first form, the presentation or image, glides

imperceptibly into the second form, that of the concept
in which the images are universalised. These are the
two moments or degrees of the theoretical activity. The
concept of each is distinct, but clearly one is not the
negation or opposite of the other—the one passes into
the other. The quality of the first moment is purely
aesthetic, and the concept of it is beauty. The quality
of the second moment is purely logical, and the concept
of it is truth.

"Two distinct concepts are united to one another
even in their distinction ; two opposite concepts seem
to exclude one another ; where the one enters, the other
totally disappears. A distinct concept is presupposed
by and lives in its other, which follows it in the ideal
order. An opposite concept is slain by its opposite : of
it the saying holds good, *mors tua, vita mea*. Examples
of distinct concepts are those just mentioned, imagination
and intellect, and we may add others, such as right,
morality, and the like. But examples of opposite
concepts are drawn from those numerous pairs of words
of which our language is full, and which are certainly not
peaceable and friendly couples. Such are the antitheses
truth and falsity, good and evil, beauty and ugliness,
worth and worthlessness, joy and sorrow, activity and
passivity, affirmation and negation, life and death, being
and nothing, and so on. It is impossible to confuse
together the two series, that of the distinct and that
of the opposite concepts, so markedly different are
they" (p. 9).

The importance of this philosophical doctrine will be
understood when we consider that upon it depends the
whole theory of the nature of error and evil. It is a
profound and far-reaching theory. The true nature of
error and evil as negations is revealed at the same time

that their full reality is recognised. The theory which denies absolutely to error and evil positive and independent reality is not a shallow optimism, such as Voltaire has satirised in *Candide*, it is a theory which resolves the dualism it has been the main effort of philosophy throughout its history to overcome. Error and evil are not independent of truth and goodness in their origin and nature, they are not the tares which an enemy has sown in the corn. They are more nearly symbolised in the old myth of the tree which God planted in paradise, by eating of whose fruit man's eyes are opened, his age of innocence ended, and he knows good and evil. It is even more strikingly illustrated if we consider the attempts of the great poets to satisfy the yearning of the religious mind to personify goodness in God. A necessity of thought has led to the personification of the negation evil in Satan. Yet the image of Satan as the poets express it is always and inevitably the image of God himself. "Satan is not a creature extraneous to God, nor yet the minister of God, he is God himself. If God had not Satan within himself he would be an abstract ideal, a mere ought to be which is not, impotent and useless" (*Logica*, p. 69). The two abstractions must be integrated, must be corrective one of the other if we would succeed in reaching the fulness of truth or of goodness.

This doctrine of the unity of opposites in the distinct or concrete concept is the dialectic. It declares that every distinct concept is a unity of opposites, each of which apart from that unity is an abstraction and unreal. The two opposites within the distinct concept are two moments of the unfolding or development or revelation, but they are synthesised from the beginning. "Taken in themselves they are not two moments bound up in a third, they are themselves one, the third (the number is only symbolical).   Hegel in his polemic against empty being was not content with the words *unity and identity*, nor with the word *synthesis*, nor with the word *triad* ; he indicated the indistinguishable opposition in the unity as the objective *dialectic* of reality.   But whatever words we choose, the fact is plain.   Opposite terms (truth and falsity, good and evil, being and nothing) are not each something distinct and complete in itself, but an abstraction from the true reality " (*Logica*, p. 68).

The distinct concept, then, is a synthesis, or unity, or identity in difference, of opposites.   It is not itself in its turn an opposite, a thesis or antithesis within a new synthesis.   And this marks Croce's departure from the Hegelian logic.   The distinct concept cannot itself be an opposite, just because in it reality is fully determined.   The distinct concept is already concrete-universal, and therefore cannot from any standpoint appear as an abstraction from reality.   It is not imperfect nor incomplete, so that it demands of thought that it should be harmonised or reconciled in a higher synthesis.   It is not the whole, but a moment in the ideal development of the whole.   There is no whole in the static sense.   Mind immanent in the concept is movement, tendency, direction ; but this activity is not the dialectic which we have seen at work in the concept, repeated again in regard to the distinct concept itself, now raised to a higher plane.   It is the twofold degree. When we reach the concepts of art and history we have done with the dialectic of opposites, we are now dealing with absolute mind.   Instead, then, of the final triad which Hegel reaches in the conclusion of the logic of the Absolute Mind,—the triad in which Art and Revealed Religion are opposites, thesis and antithesis with

Philosophy as the synthesis,—Croce presents Absolute Mind as an ideal progression of four distinct concepts. Instead of the triad we have the relation of double degree,—beauty and truth in the concrete forms of art and history, utility and goodness in the concrete forms of economic and moral conduct.

The philosophical sciences have, then, each its distinct concept, and each concept is a synthesis of opposites. There is not a science of beauty and a science of ugliness. There is one science of aesthetic.   Its concept beauty is a synthesis of opposites, the beautiful and the ugly. The same is true of truth and error, worth and worthlessness, good and evil.

CHAPTER IX

AN aesthetic fact is the presence to the mind of an object of experience, natural object or work of art, in so far as it possesses the quality or character of beauty. What is this quality of beauty? Every one is familiar with it as an experience, yet it seems mysterious and difficult, if not impossible, to define. If, however, it be difficult to give a positive content to the concept of beauty, in ordinary experience we find no difficulty in distinguishing it negatively. By beautiful we do not mean useful, and we do not mean good in the moral or ethical sense ; and though beauty may be the source or the occasion of pleasure, and its absence the occasion of displeasure, it is itself not identical with the pleasure of which it may be the occasion. There is, moreover, bewildering confusion in the application of the aesthetic judgment. No two individuals, whatever degree of culture they possess, seem able to be of one accord in their aesthetic judgment, nor does any one seem able to preserve his own individual judgment invariable. This is as true also of the general judgment as it is of the individual judgment. What once seemed beautiful and gave intense aesthetic satisfaction may come to seem ugly and be displeasing and repugnant. Hence to the ordinary man it seems that beauty can have no objective ground in fact, and in this it seems to differ from the qualities we call physical. It seems to have no necessary connexion with the reality of the world, but, on the contrary, to be merely a matter of individual and personal taste, inconstant and variable. A beautiful object gives us a distinct kind of pleasure, different from the sensual pleasure we oppose to pain ; a pleasure whose contrary is displeasure. If an object excite this particular kind of pleasure, and in so far as it does, it is beautiful. What is to one man beautiful may be to another ugly, and to the ordinary man the judgment that anything is beautiful is a matter of taste, and *de gustibus non disputandum.*

Yet there are other considerations which, even to the ordinary man, make beauty appear external to mind, that is, something objective which is not a matter of personal feeling or thinking, but inherent in reality. The chief of these is that the recognition of beauty in nature and in art is seen to be dependent on preparation in the subject. There is a work of education involving a subtle and continuous change always going on in the mind, modifying its attitude toward the beautiful object, and this supposes that there is beauty in the natural object or work of art, to be recognised. Many people, for example, derive no pleasure from listening to classical music ; many, indeed, find the experience not merely dull but a downright discomfort ; yet no one would pass the judgment that therefore classical compositions are not beautiful, nor would any one use his experience as an argument to pronounce the aesthetic judgment itself to be subjective and variable. The same is true of the other fine arts but in varying degrees.

It is not, however, in ordinary life alone and on the plane of common sense that we are confronted with inextricable confusion in the attempt to give clear and distinct meaning to our notions of the nature of our aesthetic feelings and of the objects which evoke them. Among philosophers and psychologists there is not only no agreement, but, on the contrary, the widest divergence in the varieties of aesthetic theory. Biologically, the attraction of the beautiful object and the admiration it calls forth are generally regarded as serving the function of sexual selection ; and probably, mainly on this account, beauty is by many considered to be closely associated with sexuality and a derivative of the sex instinct. For others, again, beauty is the enjoyment which accompanies the highest intellectual attainment, the satisfaction the mind obtains in the contemplation of a mystical harmony lying behind the contradictions of temporal existence.

The first essential, therefore, to a theory of beauty is to have a clear idea of the true psychological nature of our aesthetic experience. The first philosopher to make the attempt to distinguish clearly the nature of the aesthetic fact and determine its relation to the logical fact on the one hand and to the practical or ethical fact on the other was Kant. Croce recognises in the *Critique of Judgment* the real starting-point of modern scientific aesthetic theory. In enthusiastic words he compares its effect on the perplexed student of aesthetic to the joy of Dante, lost in the " oscura selva," on meeting Virgil. It is worth while, therefore, to give some attention not only to the actual aesthetic theory of Kant, but also to the circumstances which determined its form.

" The *Critique of Judgment* was published by Kant

in 1790. For a whole century before this there had been an unceasing succession of disquisitions and controversies concerning beauty, taste, genius, art. Two divergent intellectual tendencies characterised these studies. On the one hand was a tendency we may call academical, a kind of degenerate Leibnizian doctrine, represented by a minority who resolved all aesthetical facts into facts of an intellectual or moral character. On the other hand there was a majority, consisting for the most part of dilettanti and amateurs, unprejudiced if not profound, who treated aesthetic facts as pleasurable facts, more or less complicated, more or less refined. The mind of Kant, open to all forms of knowledge, could not be disinterested in problems concerning the beautiful, and from his youth he was always working at them. All his life he read and studied books and argumentative pamphlets without number. This we know from the transcriptions of his courses of lectures which have been preserved, and in which the traces of these readings are still clearly to be seen. He wavered for a time between the academical tendency and that which we may perhaps call the worldly view, but this latter appears in the end to have prevailed with him, so that at times he seemed to contemporaries to be under the direct and definite influence of the English empiricists. When in 1781 he published the first edition of the *Critique of Pure Reason*, Kant believed and definitely affirmed the empirical origin of the rules and criteria of beauty, and therefore their incapacity to be valid as laws *a priori*. In this opinion he remained for several years

" But, behold, this belief which had seemed so firm began to show signs of wavering in the beginning of 1787, and at the end of that year it had gone entirely.

In 1790 came out the *Critique of Judgment*, which
maintained the directly opposite thesis. It was a real
mental revolution which, like all revolutions, had
been slowly prepared for. This is shown by the fact
that Kant continued to use and tenaciously hold the
old argument, even after he appeared to have got rid
of it, proclaiming the non-existence of *a priori* principles
of the beautiful, or rather the impossibility of a philosophical treatment of aesthetic concepts.

" Guided by his profound consciousness of truth, he
came thus by his own indwelling force, in the face of
strong and intricate difficulties, in spite of many errors
and of many false steps, to discover, unaided, a new
continent, a new sphere of human activity, a sphere
entirely distinct from those which are commonly recognised, and which he himself had supposed to be the
only legitimate spheres. This new sphere was, so it
seemed to him, a mental realm *sui generis*, difficult to
define in a satisfactory manner, but secure and unshak-
able in the reality of its own existence, since there
flourishes in the human mind a form of judgment which
has not a logical character, and therefore is not cognitive
(if the strict meaning of cognitive be that which is
logical), and also has not a practical character (if
practical mean the existence of objects of desire). The
judgments of this particular form are accompanied by
pleasure, but not the pleasure which springs from the
lower form of appetition, that, namely, which pleases the
senses in sensation. In like manner as these judgments
exclude every volitional interest they are not moral in
character and have nothing in common with the good.
They may be defined as contemplative, but it is a contemplation which is not centred on concepts, and, accordingly,
is independent alike of the idea of external purpose or

utility, and of the idea of internal purpose or perfection.
And so far as the judgments are universal, their universality reveals itself as subjective only, devoid of an
objective criterion.   Though they are accompanied by
the feeling of approval or disapproval, they are intrinsi-
cally free from the emotions and from allurements.
This *sui generis* form, said Kant, is the form of the judgments of taste.   The facts to which these judgments
refer are beauty and art.   The productive activity which
is conjoined with them is genius, a quite different faculty
from the scientific intellect.   The usual and the most
convenient and most convincing way of dealing with
judgments of taste had been indeed to deny that they
were judgments at all, and simply to resolve them into
pleasurable feeling.   Such a sophism could not deceive
the old philosopher.   It is absurd, he exclaimed, to
deny the evidence, since the judgment of the beautiful
is separated as by an abyss from the feeling of pleasure.
It is ridiculous to say of a poem, or a symphony, or a
building on which we are asked to pass judgment, it is
beautiful ' for me.'   Things which are only pleasing
to me are things which concern me alone and not
others, but when I pronounce a judgment concerning
beauty, declaring a thing to be beautiful, I require that
others should experience the pleasure I feel.   I judge
not alone for myself but for others, and I come in this
way to discuss beauty as though it were a quality of
the thing.   When any one says, ' This thing is beautiful,' he is prepared to argue with those who judge
otherwise ;   he denies to them the taste which at the
same time he claims they ought to have.   The saying,
' Every one to his taste,' is inapplicable in the field of
aesthetic judgment, and it is contradicted at every
moment in the life of beauty and of art.

" This is Kant's discovery, and he expounds and enforces it by arguments and analyses in the first part of the *Critique of Judgment*. We may say of it that it has definitely conquered the world of the beautiful for philosophy. That world is not, even to-day, wholly surveyed and explored and described, but it remains our firm possession " (*Saggio sullo Hegel*, p. 335).

In analysing the aesthetic judgment, and in clearly distinguishing it from the logical judgment and from the practical judgment, Kant has laid down the firm basis for the superstructure of aesthetic science. It is in this foundation, not in the superstructure, that Kant's work is invaluable. " Aesthetic treatises by authors who have not studied Kant may be neglected without the least risk of serious mental loss. On the other hand, no one can stop at the *Critique of Judgment*. Kant himself would not have stopped there. Old age and death stopped him, not his will. Of his book it has often been said, that it is born of the author's indwelling force. It is not difficult to see that wherever he is most strenuous in controversy, the adversary he is combating is none other than himself, his own old beliefs and errors. This indwelling force attains its goal in the affirmation of a special aesthetic mental sphere " (p. 341).

With Kant's aesthetic theory itself, Croce does not agree. Kant is for him only one moment in the history of aesthetic, and since Kant, human thought has journeyed on and marked progress. The relation of art and philosophy in particular is never examined by Kant, so Croce declares, and it remains obscure in the *Critique of Judgment*, and it is by such examination that later aesthetic has developed.

Even when Kant, he tells us, criticising his predecessors was rejecting intellectualistic aesthetic ; when he was affirming that beauty is non-conceptual, disinterested ; purposive, but without the representation of a purpose ; source of pleasure, but of a universal pleasure ; he was readmitting intellectualism by defining a work of art as the adequate presentation of a concept, in which intellect and imagination are combined in the genius of the artist. In the end he even readmitted external finality, explaining beauty as the symbol of morality.

But there was a philosopher earlier than Kant, whom we have already had occasion to refer to, who is hailed by Croce as the real discoverer of aesthetic science. Of the intellectual wealth of this great thinker Croce always writes with enthusiasm, and he declares his own aesthetic theory to be but a rediscovery.

" The leader of the revolution in aesthetic theory, who setting aside the concept of art as verisimilitude, and giving to the faculty of imagination a new meaning, penetrated to the true nature of poetry and art, and discovered, so to say, aesthetic science, was the Italian, Giambattista Vico. In 1725 was published in Naples the first edition of his *Scienza nuova*. In 1730, a second edition with additions appeared. Their main intention was to present certain new ideas of the nature of poetry. What were these ideas ? We can now say that they are neither more nor less than the solution of the problem propounded by Plato, which Aristotle attempted to solve without success, and which has been the subject of many and various attempts from the Renascence up to our own time.—Is poetry a rational or irrational fact, is it spiritual or natural ? If it be spiritual, what is its peculiar nature, and in what is it distinguished from history and from science ? Plato,

as we know, had confined poetry to the corporeal part
of the soul, to what, in the philosophical language
of Vico's time, was termed the animal spirits. Vico
raised it up. For Vico poetry is a period in the history
of humanity,—an ideal history whose periods are not
events but forms of mind. Poetry as a moment of the
ideal history of mind is a form of consciousness, the
first to come from intellect but following after sense.
Plato, confounding it with sense, had not recognised
the place which belonged to it and had banished it
from his Republic. ' Men first *feel* without being
aware ; then they *become aware* with troubled and
affected soul ; finally, they *reflect* with pure mind.
This dignity is the *Principle of the poetical feelings*,
which are formed by the senses of *passions* and of
affections, as distinct from the *philosophical feelings*,
which are formed from *reflexion by reasoning*. Hence
the philosophical feelings approach the more to truth,
the more they rise to *universals* ; the poetical feelings
are more certain the more they approach to *particulars* ' "
(*Estetica*, p. 255. The quotation from Vico, *Scienza
nuova seconda*, *Elementi* liii.). Poetry is thus placed
on the imaginative plane as distinct from the intellective,
and this imaginative plane, or as Croce calls it degree,
is furnished with positive value.

This brief historical reference is necessary for the
full understanding of Croce's theory of Beauty, for this
rests on the affirmation of an aesthetic activity as a
special sphere of mental activity, distinct alike from the
logical activity on the one hand and from the ethical
activity on the other. Beauty is not truth and it is
not goodness, but a value distinct in its nature from
either. Beauty is successful expression. We may
even leave out the qualification " successful," and say

simply, Beauty is expression, for unsuccessful expression
is not expression.

What then is expression ? It is the form the mind
gives to its intuitions, the form intuition takes as it
utters itself. And as there is no matter without form
and no form without matter, the intuition is the
expression. This aesthetic activity is, as we have seen,
the first moment of our ideal mental history. It is the
activity of the imagination, the activity which produces
or invents or creates images, images which are particular
and individual. It is not imagination in the secondary
meaning in which it is a faculty of reproducing and
recombining fanciful images out of elements of past
experience. In its original meaning the imagination
is distinguished from the intellect as an intuition is
distinguished from a concept.

There is, however, a naturalistic meaning of the
term expression, even as applied to the work of art,
which is to be clearly distinguished from the philosophical meaning in which it is used to define beauty.
If we take an aesthetic production, say a recognised
work of fine art, we generally mean by expression
the translation of the artist's vision into physical
phenomena—colours, shapes, or sounds. It is easy to
see, however, that such naturalistic use of the term
expression is at bottom metaphorical. The true artistic
expression is never anything physical, on the contrary
it is the aesthetic mental synthesis, and it is independent
of outward translation, however necessary this translation may be for its communication. Moreover, the
naturalistic meaning of expression, even when it refers
to aesthetic facts, is not an aesthetic, nor even a
theoretical, activity, but one which is purely practical.

" When we have mastered the internal word, when

we have vividly and clearly conceived a figure or a
statue, when we have found a musical theme, expression
is born and is complete, nothing more is needed. If,
then, we open our mouth and speak or sing, the action
is voluntary, it is something we will to do, and what we
then do is say aloud what we have already said within,
sing aloud what we have already sung within. If our
hands strike the keyboard of the pianoforte, if we take
up pencil or chisel, such actions are willed, and what
we are then doing is executing in great movements
what we have already executed briefly and rapidly
within. By these actions we stamp our intuitions on a
material which will hold the traces of them more or
less enduringly. All this, however, is an added fact,
it obeys quite other laws than the aesthetic fact, it is
a production of things and therefore a *practical* or
voluntary fact. In this way we come to distinguish the
internal from the external work of art. The terminology
is unfortunate because the work of art is always and
only internal, and what is called external is no longer
the work of art " (*Estetica*, p. 58).

This metaphorical use of the term expression, to
indicate not the artist's aesthetic creation which is
purely mental, but the stamping of that creation on
physical phenomena, is embodied in our language and
thought to such an extent that it obscures and actually
falsifies the original meaning. Works of art—poems,
pictures, sculptured stone, musical compositions—are the
stimuli which evoke the reproduction in us of the
aesthetic expression, and this aesthetic expression, not
the stimulus which reproduces it, can alone in the strict
sense be termed beautiful. Beauty has no meaning
when applied to a mere physical fact, and to speak of
physical things as beautiful or of things as physically

beautiful is really to speak paradoxically. It is easy
enough to see how we come to do so. Physical facts,
being aids to the beautiful, come elliptically to be
themselves called beautiful, and in this way give rise
to the concept of physical beauty. The beautiful is
not a physical fact, beauty does not belong to things,
it belongs wholly to the human aesthetic activity, and
this is a mental or spiritual fact.

The translation of the aesthetic fact into physical
phenomena is a stage of the complete process of aesthetic
production. It is the final stage of this process, but
then the complete process of aesthetic production involves other activities besides the purely aesthetic activity,
activities which are practical or, more precisely, economic.
The pure aesthetic expression is the mental synthesis by
which man converts mere impressions into intuitions.
The giving birth to intuitions is expression. No one
will understand the theory that beauty is expression who
does not clearly grasp this essential meaning of the term.

There is yet another difficulty closely connected
with the metaphorical use of the term expression. It
requires very careful attention for it touches the pivotal
fact of the whole theory. What is ugliness? The
problem of the nature of ugliness really arises from the
application of the term beautiful to physical objects. If
we think that beauty can be a positive character of an
external work of art or of a natural object, then so
also can ugliness. We shall then be led to classify all
objects as beautiful and ugly, and perhaps also we may
distinguish a group as indifferent. Such classification,
if intended literally, must involve the denial of pure
aesthetic fact. It will follow from it that beauty and
ugliness will become general terms to indicate qualities
which produce in us a certain kind of pleasure and

displeasure, and this pleasure and displeasure will then come to be regarded as themselves the aesthetic fact. In close connexion with this metaphorical use of the term expression which makes it apply to the external physical production, there is also a very common misuse of the terms beautiful and ugly, which tends to bring utter confusion into aesthetic theory. We apply the terms beautiful and ugly to facts which belong not only to the aesthetic order, to which alone they rightly belong, but also to the other orders. In common language we are continually making this interchange. " Beautiful and ugly " express aesthetic value and its contrary ; "true and false" express logical value and its contrary; "convenient and useless " economic value and its contrary; and " good and bad " ethical value and its contrary. Yet we use the term beautiful not only for aesthetic expression, but for scientific truth, for a usefully accomplished action or for a moral action, and in this way we come to speak of intellectual beauty, of a beautiful action, of moral beauty. And the same with the contrary, the ugly, we speak of ugly truths, ugly actions, and so forth. The first requirement of philosophical theory is to recognise the order of facts to which beautiful is applicable. Pleasure and displeasure accompany the exercise of aesthetic activity, it is true, but then they also accompany all forms of mental activity ; they are not therefore themselves the aesthetic value and its contrary. The beautiful is the distinct concept of aesthetic value ; like every distinct concept it contains within it its own contrary for it is a synthesis of opposites. The beautiful, then, is aesthetic value, and aesthetic value is successful aesthetic activity, that is, expression. The ugly is spoilt expression, a shortcoming or failure to express.

Let us now try and see what this theory implies and

how it works. It affirms, and affirms with emphasis that beauty is applicable and only applicable to an active work of the mind. But it affirms more than this. When we pronounce a work of art, a poem or a picture, beautiful, the beauty concerns only the intuition which finds in the work of art expression, but this intuition is not that of an individual artist expressed once and for ever, it is the intuition of the mind which makes the aesthetic judgment. It is my intuition which finds expression in the beautiful work of art. In other words, to have aesthetic experience we must ourselves be actively creating, our own mind must be giving birth to an intuition and finding its expression, and it is that expression which is beautiful. Now it is certain this is not what we ordinarily think we mean when, let us say, we call a poem beautiful ; and it is certain we are not directly conscious of any creative act in the aesthetic judgment. Indeed, to many critics the theory has seemed so absurd, being so contrary to the whole bent of our mind, so opposite to the meaning ingrained in our thought and language, that they have not hesitated to make merry over it while rejecting it outright. We are to suppose, they say, that the great poet has intuition in a great dose, and expresses it in noble and melodious verse ; I have only a little dose and no power to compose a poem ; but my little dose of intuition is the same in kind as his, he does but help me to expression, and my expression, not the poet's verse, is what is beautiful ! So the theory is made to look absurd, but let us try and grasp its intention. The poem speaks a language to me, by which I mean not merely that it consists of words which are parts of speech, but that it communicates images and thoughts to my mind. The essential thing in language is not the material sign in physical

sound or written word but the meaning these convey.
This meaning must be meaning to me, the image must
be formed in my mind, the thought must be thought
by me, the mental activity must be my activity.   I
cannot see in a work of art another's thought save in so
far as it is my own thought.   This surely is obvious.
Why, then, can it seem absurd ?   Because we have lost
the consciousness of our aesthetic activity ; the other
activities, in particular those which are practical, and of
those which are practical, in particular those which are
economic, have so overlaid the aesthetic activity that
though it is first in the ideal history of mind, it is last
in the order of scientific discovery.   Aesthetic science is
the latest comer, the last discovery of philosophy, and
hence its importance for the whole philosophical system
of reality.

But it will still be objected that even if aesthetic
be only concerned with the internal activity in the work
of art, yet there is an external work of art, and this
must be subject to laws and therefore there must be a
science of it.   The matter the artist uses must at least
be partly subject to aesthetic science.   This, in Croce's
view, admits no compromise.   " The concept of a work
of external art is impossible even as a concept, it is for
philosophy not only serious error, it is absurdity.   The
work of art is a spiritual fact and therefore can never
be external or physical.   Statues, pictures, poems,
symphonies can be weighed, measured, and counted, like
other physical things, but to the physicists who may so
treat them they are external things and entirely without
spiritual meaning.   For the aesthetician there exist no
things which are measured, weighed, and counted, there
exist only images, mental acts.   To attempt to find a
passage or connexion between the spirituality of the

image and the physical complexes of colours, sounds, and words is a desperate enterprise. The internal expression is indeed both a movement and a physically constructible fact. But to know the nature of things comes not within the scope of physics, which is limited, so to say, to the arithmetic of them. For physics is physics only, not philosophy as well. The scope and purpose of the philosophical science aesthetic is precisely this—to attain to the nature of the expressive function. It follows, therefore, that it is impossible to make use of the non-philosophical categories of physics in regard to any aesthetic problem or inquiry whatsoever " (*Problemi di Estetica*, p. 467, part of the reply to a criticism of his theory by Prof. Faggi).

Clear though the central truth of this position may be, it seems to leave an unsatisfactory residue of doubt and difficulty. Why, it may be asked, should this passage from the internal to the external, from the mental image to the physical complex of colours, tones, and lines, be a "desperate enterprise" (*impresa desperata*)? Is there not something paradoxical, or rather, shall we not be inclined to say, something stultifying, in declaring philosophy to be science of mind, and mind to be the whole reality, and then rejecting some reality as wholly outside philosophy?

Before I try to give the answer, let me examine the difficulty more closely, for it touches the very crucial point of the theory, and the character which distinguishes it as aesthetic. The expressionist theory in effect rejects as absurdity the whole notion of a physical beauty, whether it be of a work of art or of a natural object. Moreover, it declares that it is just the tacit, unconscious, and unchallenged acceptance of this concept of physical beauty which underlies all the contradictions and paradoxes of other theories, whether they be popular or philosophical. An illustration may make my meaning plain. Suppose we affirm, as has been affirmed, that there is an actual physical beauty of the human form, meaning that the colours, tones, and general delineaments of the human form, and a particular proportion and relation of them, have aesthetic value, beauty. In that case a certain combination of purely physical characters is beautiful, a different combination is ugly. How, then, are we going to decide between the aesthetic judgment of, say, a Teuton and a Japanese in a particular case? Plainly, we cannot if we appeal to anything physical. If we cannot, how can there be a physical aesthetic criterion? On the other hand, the moment we reject this concept of a physical beauty and make appeal to the internal image, universal agreement in aesthetic judgment becomes a possibility. But then, again, if we reject the physical as external from the aesthetic activity as internal our difficulty is not at an end, indeed it may be said to be only beginning, for there will stand over against us a foreign, even hostile, world which we must go forth to conquer, for we have to make of this external physical the instrument of the mind's activity, the means by which we communicate our aesthetic expression, the beautiful. And this problem merges itself into the larger problem, the problem of these two orders of reality, the physical and the psychical and their relation—the problem of soul and body.

Let us return, however, to the question in the form which we first raised it. How and in what manner can there be a reality outside philosophy? The answer is that in one sense only can there be outside reality. Philosophy is *scientia qualitatum*, and in that signification it is science of reality. It is only as abstract and when considered in its abstractness that anything is outside philosophy. In this sense the reality which is studied in physical science is outside philosophy.

The problem, therefore, assumes for me this form. (I say assumes for me, because I am now presenting it and expressing it in my own terms. The view I am about to put forward seems to me to express Croce's doctrine, but I cannot give references and do not know that he would accept my interpretations.) Reality may be studied in two ways, and according to which of these we adopt the whole aspect of reality alters. One is the way of science, the other is the way of philosophy. The reality is one and identical, but for philosophy reality is the mind's activity, a concrete whole in which every part is in intimate and interdependent organic relation with every other part, and in which no part can be separated from the whole, of which it forms a part, without losing its meaning. Physical science studies reality as it is viewed externally by the mind, that is, as it appears to the mind when the mind sets it over against itself and presents it to itself as its object. This it can only do by an act of abstraction which is deliberate. Reality by this act is made to appear to consist of parts which are separate and separable one from another, and the whole is no more than the aggregate of the parts.

This appears to me to reconcile completely the apparent contradiction that there can be a reality outside philosophy, and that the passage from the internal image to the outside material is a " desperate enterprise." For philosophy as Science stands to physics, chemistry, biology, and the rest of the sciences, in a wholly unique relation. There is no passage from one to the other, for they deal with reality under mutually exclusive aspects. What, then, are the sciences? To this question Croce gives us the answer, They are productions of the economic activity of the mind. The pragmatic principle applies to them absolutely. They are justified in as much as and in so far as they work. They serve the practical activity of man's life. So regarded they are of course brought back one and all within philosophy, but only by casting away their essential character of abstractness which gives them their scientific value.

It is in this meaning that we can put the question concerning aesthetic, Is it philosophy or is it science? And it is clear the answer will be that it is one or the other, according to whether the aesthetic value, beauty, is applicable to a physical object or not.

The expressionist theory is that beauty is aesthetic value, and aesthetic is a philosophical science. Aesthetic is a mental activity, and the activities which are distinguished in philosophy are not parts of mind which can be abstracted or separated from the organic unity of the whole, and still retain their essential character. They are distinctions within a unity which is indivisible, and in which all differences are in organic relation of interdependence on one another. Aesthetic, therefore, although a distinct activity, a moment in an ideal history, is not independent of the other activities which constitute the unity of the life of mind.

The expressionist theory, on the other hand, is wholly incompatible with the view that aesthetic is a natural or physical science, or that it can find a place among the sciences of external reality. The sciences rest on abstract concepts and consist of abstract systems which are mutually exclusive. The unity of the sciences is not an organic but a mechanical unity. Their method is descriptive and classificatory. Now suppose that into this mechanical system of descriptive and classified facts we wish to introduce a science of beautiful objects. Where shall we place it? The incongruity is obvious. It would be like having a science of the marks which form letters and express meanings, and another science of the marks which express no meanings. In the first place, one science would not suffice, for if there are physical objects which are beautiful, there are physical objects which are ugly. Shall we not also have to add a science of physical objects which are indifferent? Beauty, therefore, in the expressionist theory is no more inherent in the physical object we are accustomed to call beautiful than meaning is inherent in the printed word. Beauty, like meaning, is the expression which is wholly and only mental.

CHAPTER X

WHEN we compare Croce's concept of Philosophy as the perfect or completed science of Mind with the concepts of other philosophers, one thing may strike us as a remarkable omission. The religious activity has no place in it. There is no recognition of a realm of religion side by side with a realm of art and a realm of intellect or logic in the theoretical sphere, neither in the practical sphere is a religious action recognised as distinct from an ethical action and from an economic action. There are, as we have seen, four forms of the mental life, four moments in its ideal history, and other forms than these, other moments than these there are none. These four pure forms, the aesthetic, the logical, the economic, and the ethical, complete reality, not in the sense that they exhaust its infinite variety, but that they exhibit the mental activity in its perfect organic unity. There are many claimants, but among the rejected none is so important as religion. What, then, in Croce's view is the religious activity? It is for him a hybrid activity, partaking now of aesthetic, now of logic. Religion is mythology, and mythology is in part art and in part philosophy. Though this may sound to many an irreverent doctrine, it is not necessarily so. It involves nothing derogatory to religion. To deny that we can differentiate religious activity as a pure form of the mental life is not to deny religion, rather is it to affirm that for some, art, for others, philosophy, is religion. And that is as much as to say that any activity raised to a higher dignity may become religion.

" Where there is no knowledge there is no religion, and religion is not a form of knowledge distinguished from other forms, for it is sometimes an expression of practical aspirations and ideals, sometimes a historical narrative, sometimes a conceptual science, dogmatic theology. With equal cogency, then, we may maintain both that religion is destroyed by the progress of human knowledge and that it always persists in that progress. To primitive peoples religion was the whole patrimony of knowledge ; to us our patrimony of knowledge is our religion. Its content has changed, has ameliorated, has become refined ; in the future it will contrive to change, to be ameliorated, to be refined, but its form does not change, that is always the same. How those who would preserve religion as a theoretical human activity side by side with art and philosophy would use it, I do not know. It is not possible to preserve an imperfect and inferior knowledge side by side with the knowledge which has gone beyond it and invalidated it. Catholicism, always consistent, tolerates neither a science, nor a history, nor an ethic, which contradicts its own views and doctrines. Rationalists are less consistent, they like to leave a little room in the soul for a religion in contradiction with their whole theoretical world " (*Estetica*, p. 73).

In denying that there is a pure form of activity, different from art and different from philosophy, manifesting itself in religion, the question of religious truth or falsity, so far as it concerns any particular belief, whether of historical fact or of theological dogma, is not raised. There is a very commonly held opinion, not confined to the vulgar, but an essential part of many philosophical systems, that religion is an experience *sui generis*, a pure spiritual life, distinct from intuition and from thought, from imagination and from intellect, a direct communion of the soul unmediated by sensible imagery or by ideas. Croce rejects this, and its rejection is an essential part of his theory of art and philosophy. Art is vision or intuition, philosophy is concept, and there is no third form of mind.

It has no doubt to be borne in mind that in his polemic against religion Croce has chiefly in view the form of religion which is represented by Catholicism. It may be thought that an Italian philosopher has special reasons for hostility to Catholicism quite apart from philosophical criticism, and that wherever there is hostility there is almost of necessity prejudice, and prejudice must affect the philosophical judgment. Had Croce come into direct contact with the more spiritual forms of religion, even of Catholicism, to be met with in some of the Protestant countries, might not his view have been greatly modified ? While it is true that much of his argument against recognising a pure form of mind in religion derives its main force from considerations which specially apply to Catholicism, I do not think the argument itself is affected by this. The essential charge against religion is, as I shall try to show, that religion is a philosophy of history. This applies to every form of Christianity, Catholic and Protestant, to the Lutheran as much as to the Thomist. It does not, I admit, apply to mystical systems in which an interpretation of history or a historical revelation has no place, although even such a conception of religion does not escape the consequence of the argument. The argument is however itself mainly directed against the Hegelian doctrine of Religion as a form of Absolute Mind. Hegel leaves no doubt of what he intends by religion. He terms it Revealed Religion (*die geoffen-bärte Religion*), and the revelation is historical, and takes its place in his system as the antithesis of art.

In the last chapter I showed how, in Croce's view, Kant after he had attained a true theory of Aesthetic, fell away from it in his attempt to formulate a theory of art. He conceived art according to a formula accepted in his time, as "the sensible and imaginative clothing of an intellectual concept." For Kant art is not *pure beauty*, quite separate from the concept, but *adherent beauty* which supposes a concept, and is fixed in regard to it. "Natural beauty (*Naturschönheit*)," he says, "is a beautiful thing; artistic beauty (*Kunstschönheit*) is a beautiful presentation of a thing" (*Kritik der Urtheils-kraft*, § 48).

In Kant, therefore, we find a theory of beauty distinct from a theory of art. In defining beauty he came to affirm a domain of mental activity distinct from the pleasant, the useful, and the good on the one hand, and from the true on the other. "The beautiful," he said, "is what pleases without interest," and also "the beautiful is what pleases without a concept." But art is definitely allotted to the concept, and the domain of beauty is a special sentimental activity named aesthetic judgment.

The ground of this theory, Croce tells us, is obvious when we study Kant's system. In his philosophy of mind there is no place among the "faculties" for the creative or inventive imagination. Genius was not such a faculty, it was the result of a co-operation of several faculties. Kant, indeed, recognises a reproductive imagination and a combining imagination, but not an imagination productive of images in the true sense. In the table of all the faculties in their systematic unity, which he prefixed to the *Critique of Judgment*, there is a cognitive faculty to which Understanding or Intellect corresponds, the feeling of pleasure and displeasure to which the Judgment (aesthetic and teleological) corresponds, and the faculty of desire to which Reason corresponds. Imagination remains outside or behind among the facts of sensation.

Let us set against this Croce's theory of Art. Art is intuition. It is a distinct form of knowledge and that the most immediate form. " It is the dream stage of life which is followed by the waking stage, when image and lyrical expression no longer suffice, and concept and judgment are needed. Without the imagery there can be no thought, but thought takes possession of the image, includes it within itself, transforms it into perception, and so gives to the dream world of art the sharp distinctions and firm outlines of reality. Art cannot of itself achieve this. All our love of art cannot raise its degree, any more than our love of a beautiful child can raise it to manhood " (*Problemi di Estetica*, p. 29).

Theory of Art, Philosophy of Art, fill a large place in the development which followed Kant. It forms a very important part of the philosophy of Hegel. Art is there brought into direct relation with Religion. Hegel places art and religion within the sphere of Absolute Mind, and they stand as thesis and antithesis with Philosophy as the synthesis in the highest triad. In accordance with his dialectical principle, Religion is posited as the negation of Art, with which also it is identical.

"It is no doubt the case," Hegel says in the Introduction to the *Aesthetik* (I quote Mr. Bosanquet's translation, p. 48), "that art can be employed as a fleeting pastime, to serve the ends of pleasure and entertainment, to decorate our surroundings, to impart pleasantness to the external conditions of our life, and to emphasise other objects by means of ornament. In this mode of employment art is indeed not independent, not free, but servile. But what *we* mean to consider is the art which is *free* in its end as in its means.

"Fine art is not real art till it is in this sense free, and only achieves its highest task when it has taken its place in the same sphere with religion and philosophy, and has become simply a mode of revealing to consciousness and bringing to utterance the Divine Nature (*das Göttliche*), the deepest interests of humanity, and the most comprehensive truths of the mind. It is in works of art that nations have deposited the profoundest intuitions and ideas of their hearts ; and fine art is frequently the key—with many nations there is no other—to the understanding of their wisdom and of their religion.

"This is an attribute which art shares with religion and philosophy, only in this peculiar mode, that it represents even the highest ideas *in sensuous forms*, thereby bringing them nearer to the character of natural phenomena, to the senses, and to feeling. The world, into whose depths *thought* penetrates, is a supra-sensuous world, which is thus, to begin with, erected as a *beyond* over against immediate consciousness and present sensation ; the power which thus rescues itself from the *here*, that consists in the actuality and finiteness of sense, is the freedom of thought in cognition. But the mind is able to heal this schism which its advance creates ; it generates out of itself the works of fine art as the first middle term of reconciliation between pure thought and what is external, sensuous, and transitory, between nature with its finite actuality, and the infinite freedom of the reason that comprehends."

Let us consider, side by side with this, the definition of Religion with which the Introduction to the *Philosophy of Religion* opens. Here Hegel declares that religion is *free* in the same absolute sense, and that it is a mode of consciousness on the highest level, that is, belonging to the absolute sphere of mind. (I quote the English translation by Speirs and Sanderson.) " We know that in religion we withdraw ourselves from what is temporal, and that religion is for our consciousness, that region in which all the enigmas of the world are solved, all the contradictions of deeper-reaching thought have their meaning unveiled, and where the voice of the heart's pain is silenced— the region of eternal truth, of eternal rest, of eternal peace. Speaking generally, it is through thought, concrete thought, or, to put it more definitely, it is by reason of his being Spirit (*Geist*) that man is man ; and from man as Spirit proceed all the many developments of the sciences and arts, the interests of political life, and all those conditions which have reference to man's freedom and will. But all these manifold forms of human relations, activities, and pleasures, and all the ways in which these are intertwined, all that has worth and dignity for man, all wherein he seeks his happiness, his glory, and his pride, finds its ultimate centre in religion, in the thought, the consciousness, and the feeling of God. Thus God is the beginning of all

things, and the end of all things. As all things proceed from this point, so all return back to it again.
He is the centre which gives life and quickening to all
things, and which animates and preserves in existence
all the various forms of being. In religion man places
himself in a relation to this centre, in which all other
relations concentrate themselves, and in so doing he
rises up to the highest level of consciousness, and to
the region which is free from relation to what is other
than itself, to something which is absolutely self-
sufficient, the unconditioned, what is free, and is its
own object and end."

The whole Hegelian philosophy may be said to be the
affirmation of a concrete concept, unknown to common
sense, and to scientific thought. The concepts of
science and of common sense are one-sided aspects of
reality, or abstract determinations of reality, and they
exhibit contradictions and inconsistencies which are
due entirely to their one-sided and abstract character.
Because of their contradictions and inconsistencies the
human mind cannot rest satisfied with them, and is
driven by its own living activity to seek a reconciliation. This force of the living activity of thought is
the dialectic. But the concrete concept, what Hegel
terms the notion or the absolute Idea, is not a construction of thought. It is the reality to which philosophy
introduces us straightway, and which it makes its
special study. This concrete concept is itself manifested in moments, and the moments are themselves
subject to the same dialectical process, a process which
characterises thought in all its manifestations, the higher
as well as the lower. Croce, as we have already seen,
dissents from this doctrine. In his view the movement
of thought whose object is the concrete concept, is not

dialectical, moving through negation to reconciliation and unity, it is a movement from a first to a second degree. The definite application of this philosophical doctrine is seen, first, in the denial that there is a special form of activity, religion, and, secondly, in the denial that religion is the negation of art, and the stage of a higher unity, philosophy.

The theory that art is intuition, vision, really means that art is entirely devoid of the character of conceptual knowledge. Intuition knows no distinction between real and unreal, it accepts the simple image at its face value. Conceptual knowledge, on the other hand, in its pure, that is, its philosophical form, rests on the distinction between reality and unreality. Its aim is to set up reality in place of unreality, or to abase unreality by showing it to be a subordinate moment of reality. In opposing intuitive or sensible knowledge to conceptual or intelligible knowledge, aesthetic to noetic, we are claiming that the simpler and more elementary form is autonomous. If art belong to this simpler form then to ask in regard to a work of art whether what the artist has expressed is metaphysically and historically true or false, is as senseless as it would be to bring the airy images of fancy before a moral tribunal. Why is it senseless ? Because the discrimination, true and false, always concerns an affirmation of reality, or a judgment, it can have nothing to do with the presentation of an image or with a mere subject, which is not the subject of a judgment, and of which neither qualification nor predicate is affirmed. If it be objected that the individuality of the image cannot subsist without reference to the universal of which it is the individualisation, this is not denied, on the contrary, it is the very principle of the twofold degree. What is denied is that the universal is logically explicit in the pure intuition, that the intuition itself is thought.

The inner force of art is ideality. It is this character which distinguishes the intuition from the concept, art from philosophy, that is, from the affirmation of the universal, and from history, that is, from the perception or narration of an event. No sooner does reflection and judgment develop from that ideality than art dies. It dies in the artist who from being artist becomes critic, it dies in the contemplator whose rapt enjoyment changes to pensive observation of life.

This, then, is the ground of Croce's rejection of Hegel's aesthetic theory. For Hegel the form of art is a veil, the reality, the Idea which it clothes. Beauty and truth are distinct and at the same time one. The true is the Idea as Idea, in its universal principle, thought. But the Idea must become actual externally and acquire a definite affective existence. This sensible appearance of the Idea is the beautiful. For Croce, on the contrary, art is pure intuition, and intuition a moment of mind devoid of conceptual form.

The distinction between art and philosophy that art is alogical, devoid of conceptual knowledge and therefore of the contrast between reality and unreality, while philosophy involves this distinction, makes clear what Croce intends when he declares religion to be mythology. " The myth presents itself to the believer as revelation, as a knowledge of the reality opposed to the unreality, it is the rejection of other beliefs as illusory and false. To the believer the myth is not art. It can only become art to one who no longer believes it, for whom mythology is valuable as a metaphor, for whom the divine world is the beautiful world, and God the image of sublimity.

Considered in its genuine, reality, as it exists in the believers' mind who has never known doubt, the myth is religion and not simply imaginative form. To such a one religion is philosophy, philosophy elaborated and more or less imperfect, but still philosophy, just as philosophy is religion more or less purified and elaborated, in continual process of elaboration and purification, but still religion, the thought of the absolute and of the eternal. What is lacking in art is precisely the thought and the faith generated by it, and this belongs to the myth and to religion. The artist does not believe nor disbelieve his images, he produces them" (*Breviario di Estetica*, p. 28).

This brings us to Croce's main argument against the Hegelian theory of religion. It is that the religion therein opposed to art is not in the true sense religion, but a certain theological construction which poses as the Philosophy of History. This for Croce is a false idea, involving a false concept of history and a false concept of philosophy. The fundamental idea which underlies it is that the course of secular events is not an intrinsic and objective development but a development overruled by final causes which are not immanent in the history but the manifestation of a mind transcending history. Philosophy of history is found in ancient as well as in modern philosophy, but in Christianity it became a perfected body of doctrine. Its purest philosophical form we find in St. Augustine, in the concept of the *Civitas Dei* struggling against *Civitas terrena* or *Civitas Diaboli*. The whole content of Christianity is a philosophy of history. The birth of Jesus Christ is for Christianity the central historical fact towards which all previous events from the creation of man are seen to converge and from which all subsequent events derive their only true meaning. And this Christian conception has dominated philosophy and identified itself with philosophy throughout the long period which divides the modern from the ancient thought.

Philosophy of History is not of course identical with Christianity. It existed for the Greeks in their concept of Fate, or Fortune, or Chance. Their historians, even when free from theological prepossessions, treated history as a great drama of the play of spiritual forces. Some like Plutarch found the chief value of historical records to be their ethical teaching. In the Hebrew writings history is simply the record of a providence overruling events. It is in this form that religion stands opposed to art and at the same time identical with it. A concrete illustration of its effect on art criticism is Ruskin's description of Tintoretto's paintings in the Scuola di San Rocco. He reads into the historical events, which form the subject-matter of the painter's pictures, the moral lessons of those events, and he represents the greatness of the artist as consisting in his power to discern and suggest ethical meanings.

Even now for those who have entirely abandoned the theology and teleology of the age of authority and dogmatism, this conception of a philosophy of history still survives clothed in other forms. The latest of these, says Croce, is a form which has lived out its life in our own days, the materialistic conception of history of Karl Marx, the philosopher of Socialism " who proclaimed a new God, Economy, and conceived the history of the human race as the expulsion from the garden of Eden of primitive communism and the effort to regain an entry into it after an age-long struggle of the classes, by the restoration of a higher and more reflective communism " (*Speech in the Senate*, May 29, 1913).

The whole force of Croce's polemic against religion conceived as a pure form of mind to be ranked with art and philosophy in the final triad is that it is essentially the concept of a transcendent and not of an immanent life. For this reason, and not for any irreverent reason, he rejects religion and relegates it to mythology. Religion is an imperfect and immature attempt to present reality, and it must therefore yield its place to philosophy. The great philosophical task before us to-day, Croce tells us, is the casting off of this worn-out garment, and this will be accomplished by the rejection of the concept of a philosophy of history and its replacement with the concept of history as identical with philosophy.

In this conception of history, in which philosophy is immanent and not transcendent, in which philosophy is history and not of history, in which the philosopher is really the writer of history, we come on Croce's central idea and fundamental principle. This I will try to expound in the next chapter. There are, however, some objections to the general view of religion which cannot be passed unnoticed.

The theory that religion is an inferior philosophy which resolves itself into philosophy proper may arouse protest, and the protest may take different forms. It will be said by some that the religion which Croce refuses to recognise as a pure form of mind is a mythology which pictures God as a being apart from the world of his creation, interfering providentially in its history, in order to convey to finite minds the revelation of his power and of his goodness. To many people this is a gross and childish concept, and

philosophers have set aside childish things. Is there
not for philosophy a profounder sense of the term
religion to denote the reverence and awe, or, it may be,
the sympathy and love we experience in the contemplation of the mystery of the universe, and in our feeling
of participation in the evolution of its life? This, it
will be said, persists in those for whom no trace of a
transcendent theory remains. No mythology, in any
recognisable form, it will be urged, enters into or
supports this experience, and many can bear abundant
testimony to its reality and to the specific form of its
existence.

Croce's reply would be, I imagine, that in so far as
this experience claims to be cognitive, it is not another
form of theoretical activity to be ranged side by side
with aesthetic and logic, while the extent to which
it is free from the cruder kind of imagery is a
question of degree. A religion which can maintain
its theoretic form is a philosophy which has not
emerged from mythology. The mind has fashioned for
itself idols and fetiches, and these remain distinctive of
religion however refined they may be when compared
with the more familiar primitive forms.

The protest may, however, take another form. It
may be said that religion in its profound meaning is
not a form of knowledge but rather a practical attitude
of mind. Religion means the fear of God, adoration
of God, and hope in God, and it is one and the same
whatever be the precise meaning we put into the
concept God, and whether it be the concept of a transcendent or of an immanent reality.

Croce is aware of this objection. " It cannot be
denied that the doctrine which resolves religion into
philosophy, which considers it as a kind of *inferior*

philosophy, proves sometimes and in a subtle way un-satisfactory even to those who have fully accepted the concept of reality as immanence ; and the dissatisfac-tion, if it be carefully observed, is almost always due to the fact that the word philosophy conveys no idea of what actually characterises the religious life, namely, adora-tion, the fear of God, awe, and hope. Hence the protest that religion is a practical and not a theoretical, or not a purely theoretical, form." This dissatisfaction arises, he goes on to argue, from the failure to see that religion is not in a merely general way a lower form of philosophy, but one particular lower form of it, that characterised by mythology (*il mitolo-gismo*). In every department of thought there is a tendency in the mind to personify concepts. " It is at first metaphorical, but metaphors become objectified into idols of the imagination until life comes to be presented not as it is, the reality of human thought and action, but rather as a drama of feeling and action in which personified concepts are the actors. Philosophy seems then to come and dissolve these idols, diffusing, as it were, a cold wind over a world already full of the warm breath of life. But the idols are dear to us just because they are idols, that is, images of things we hold dear; dear, too, in their way are the idols which represent the contrary of those images we cherish and venerate, for the being of these images of evil is dialectically involved in the being of the good. The devil makes us feel the power of God, and doubt of the devil undermines our belief in God. It is quite natural, therefore, that philosophy when it criticises religion and itself completes its imperfection and shortcoming, so taking its place, should not only bring affliction to the mind, but make the heart bleed.

And philosophy comes to be cursed in prose, and above all in poetry, by many souls tormented at the death of their gods, the loss of their idols, and who can find no adequate consolation in the new ideal world—home-sick souls to whom purity of ideas will never be compensation for loss of cherished images. And, indeed, there is no one, however he may have freed himself from the religious beliefs once cared for, who does not retain in his soul some tenderness for the fallen idols." " In religious mythology there are not only hedonistic idols, but also cosmical explanations, the wealth and importance of which, enveloped in mythological form, present the measure of the progress of religions and of their successive approximations to philosophy. On the other hand, they cannot pass into and be fused in philosophy by insensible degrees, but only through a spiritual revolution by which the will is purified of every material residue, egoistic or eudemonistic ; by which also the religious thoughts and images are stripped of their transcendent or mythological character, made to renounce the sensible attraction of these garments and are transfigured into ideas ; not cold, as is believed, but limpid and serene, springs of pure joy " (*Critica*, vol. xv. p. 67).

The rejection of Religion as a pure form of mind and distinct moment in its ideal development follows therefore from the uncompromising application of the philosophical principle of immanence. To many philosophers, among them some of the greatest, it has seemed that an immanent God is not God. It was philosophers who charged Spinoza with atheism. To those, however, who accept the immanent principle without reservation, philosophy does not dethrone religion, it becomes religion.

CHAPTER XI

THE CONCEPT OF HISTORY

HISTORY is the most concrete form in which reality is presented to consciousness. History, therefore, in the form of judgment, that is, not in the form of particular narrative but in the form of judgment of fact, historical judgment, is the highest form of philosophy itself and identical with it. This implies that the events which make up the course of history are in their nature ideal; they are the expression of mental activity; nothing which is in the true sense history is extrinsic to mind. (I use the term "history" to denote both the literary form, what Croce terms "Historiography," and also the material content. We are accustomed to this use and I do not think it leads to confusion.)

History is ordinarily conceived as a record of the past, and the past is conceived as something which is over and done with, as what has existed or what did exist but which is now non-existent, dead. The philosophical concept of history is altogether different. History is present reality. It exists in the actual present in the same way in which the full reality of the individual past exists in the present moment of an individual consciousness. The past is not an external condition of the present; it is not a cause which has ceased to exist except in so far as the present is its mechanical effect. To the philosopher history is present existence, and universal history is to reality what to each individual his own particular history is to the reality he names self. The unreflective man, it is true, conceives himself not as being history but as having a history. He conceives himself as an entity which has lived through a certain objective series of events, external to him, and independent of him, but reacting upon him ; and also he supposes that he in his turn has reacted on events, causing them to be different than they would otherwise have been. Yet, whenever we contemplate this soul, or mind, or self, and try to imagine it apart from its history, we find that we are trying to conceive the inconceivable, and are giving substance to a pure abstraction. Our mind is not something outside its history. We are what we have been, our history is our reality. The truth of this is hidden from us, however, in life, and we are the subjects of a persistent illusion. The illusion is due to the momentary character of our consciousness, and consists in attributing to reality itself the sharp distinction which confines our consciousness of reality to the actual span of duration which in experience we call now. Reality seems to us an existing present which has succeeded a non-existing past, a past which did exist but does not exist, and which is confronted with a non-existing future, a future which will exist but does not now exist. But, as has been often pointed out, such a conception when pressed to its logical conclusion leaves nothing to the present but a mathematical instant with no dimension, and, therefore, with nothing to exist. Past, present, and future are, however, necessary parts of the conception of every actual activity, or change, or process, or life. The past is acted, it is in that sense unalterable, but its determination is the present in which it acts. The past is an absolutely essential part of the present in the sense that cut off from it the present loses all meaning and content. The future is equally essential, it is the yet undetermined, the actual possibility, which is a necessary part of the concept of every present process or change.

In individual experience, then, the present is not a mathematical point but a duration span. There is no point dividing existence from non-existence. The illusion that there is such a division is due to the momentary character of consciousness. It is conscious-ness, however, which is momentary, and the illusion is persistent because of our power to measure this moment by means of a material or spatial clock. We find that the moment coincides with a definite period of clock time. This limit of the duration of the moment appears to be specific and also to subserve a biological purpose. It is probable that it varies greatly in different species, but in any case it is purely subjective, characterising consciousness or awareness, confining it to fixed attention at the centre of living action. In other words, the relation of before and after in the present duration span of an individual experience is not a distinction of what exists from what does not exist. All the duration it embraces exists, and the span itself is (theoretically) without limit. (I have further developed this argument in a paper on " The Moment of Experience," *Proceedings of the Aristotelian Society*, vol. xvi.)

This is not Croce's argument, nor is it the way in which he has presented his theory of the identity of history and philosophy. I have chosen to set it forth in this way because it seems to me that the truth of the theory wholly depends on our recognition that reality, or mind, is the kind of continuity we name duration.

Before we examine the special problem to which the concept of history gives rise, let us first understand the place it occupies in the general scheme of Croce's philosophy. The work of philosophy is not complete when we have distinguished the different forms of knowledge and shown their relation. Such work is an essential and necessary part of philosophy, but it is only preliminary to the study of philosophy proper, just as the dissection of the body is necessary if we would understand the structure and function of the various organs; but philosophy requires us to go beyond this necessary preliminary and study the mind, as in physiology we must study the body, in its living process as an individual whole.

The study of the living mind, or of the life of mind, is exactly analogous to the study of the bodily life. We first form a system or scheme of it, and then by the aid of this scheme we present to ourselves the living process in its indivisible unity. But this unity of living process is not merely the perfect model set in action. No scheme which thought can attain to is adequate to mind itself. The life is more than the movement and more than the functioning of the parts. Even the two fundamental forms of mind, the theoretical and the practical, knowing and acting, are not numerically two, nor are they merely co-ordinated forms. Each is in the other, and each presupposes the other.

There is, then, a knowing of mind or reality in its fulness or life, and there are forms of this knowing. It is a little difficult to express these two kinds of

knowing because we have allowed the verb which
corresponds to the noun wisdom to drop into disuse,
and therefore our language does not, as the Italian or
French does, enable us to distinguish *conoscere* and
sapere, connaître and *savoir* ; one word *know* has to serve
us for both. But we have the word wisdom, and if we
choose to use it in its original meaning, we may say
that besides the forms of knowledge, aesthetic and
logic, there are forms of wisdom, art and history.
The difference is that in the forms of wisdom as
compared with the forms of knowledge we are not
aiming at something pure, but at presenting reality in
the full concreteness of its life, the mind, as it were,
not in its abstract moments but in the full course
of its flesh and blood activity. It is not only the
distinction, so frequently drawn between a formal logic
and an applied logic, between a pure aesthetic and an
applied aesthetic, it is rather the difference between
philosophy and art in their full comprehensiveness,
in which each is the whole, and unites within itself all
the activity of the mind. This full concrete reality of
actual life is conceived by us either statically in art
or dynamically in history. In history we lose all
distinction between thought and reality, between
purposes and events, between mind and body, and
show the actual unfolding of the full reality as an
indwelling life expressing itself in action, and the
highest form of philosophy is therefore history.

The act of thinking is always philosophy and history
at one and the same time ; history is, in fact, identical
with the act of thinking itself. This is the fundamental position of Croce's doctrine of history. It is
not self-evident, and, indeed, the popular notion of
history is the direct contrary of it. The ordinary

notion of history is that it deals with events which are altogether distinct and independent of acts of thinking. It is popularly thought that there are events and that there may be a pure chronicle of them, a chronicle of occurrences devoid of any character or meaning. When events are past we are dependent for the history of them on the documents and traditions which testify to them, and these may require ingenuity to interpret ; this is the work of the historian, and in performing it we think of him as best qualified to be successful when he is most disinterested and dispassionate. The popular notion, therefore, supposes that there are events of which it can be said that their existence is independent of all interpretation, and that the work of the historian is to select them for their extrinsic interest or importance. It would be a purposeless task to record everything and so reduplicate experience, but there is nothing, it is thought, theoretically impossible in the idea. The historian, we say, should have nothing to do with meaning and purpose, which are entirely extrinsic to the events, and, therefore, it would seem the philosopher, who is only concerned with these, ought to be the least qualified to interpret history.

Croce's concept of history is the very reverse of this. History is the form in which the full reality of existence is presented to consciousness. History is not the story of life but the story immanent in the fact that life is an unfolding and expression. History presents to us life or mind in its reality, and, therefore, history and philosophy are in their essence identical (*Logic*, part ii. chap. iv.).

This view of the identity of philosophy and history involves several positions which are, to the ordinary

notion of what history is, paradoxical. It involves the
doctrine that all history is contemporaneous history.
It involves also the doctrine that the determination of
an event, that which gives it its historical character,
is an immanent principle. There exist no events
external to history, independent of history, dead material
of history, forming the objective substratum of a con-
structive or reconstructive work. There are, that is
to say, no facts without meaning to which the mind
can add any meaning. Let us first look at these
propositions which seem paradoxes to the popular mind.
I will begin with the second as being the most directly
opposite to the general opinion.

It is easy to see how the notion of unhistorical
events arises. I walk through a country churchyard
and read the inscriptions graven on the tombstones.
Here I seem to have in its simplest form the popular
distinction between the independent matter which
history is concerned with and the external form which
history assumes. The bare record is the history, the
individual life to which the inscription refers, and of
which but for the record there is no history, is the
matter. But bare records are not history, they are
documents for the historian, and guide him to the
history ; and the events they record have no self-
subsistence, they are only historical to the extent the
mind can enter them and think them as belonging to
concrete universal life. To be historical is not to be
reproduced in a truthful record which reflects as a
mirror or preserves as a photograph the scene enacted,
it is to enter integrally into the actual universal life
which is reality. Our language, too, preserves this
meaning, as when we speak of an historical personage.
The notion of a succession of objective events

independent of human thought and action and forming
the substratum of history, however certain it may seem
to unreflective thought, may easily be shown to lead to
absurdity. It is really the same notion which has given
rise to that will-o'-the-wisp of philosophy, the notion of
the thing-in-itself. Applied to the concept of history,
however, its meaninglessness is more immediately
evident. Deprive an event of its meaning, that is,
deprive it entirely of the spiritual character which
connects it with human action, leave it its bare existence
as fact,—movement of physical elements, or abstract
mathematical relations,—and you take from it everything which constitutes history, everything distinctive
of history, you leave nothing which for a historian is
anything. It is not possible to abstract from concrete
human activity its physical and mathematical aspects,
and regard these as the natural and mathematical
sciences do, as independent realities, and at the same
time retain in them the character which makes history.
It is purely human purpose, theoretical and practical
activity, mind, which is the reality the science of history
deals with. The matter of history is the enduring,
continuous life of mind.

It will be objected, however, that history is not life
but the record of life, and this record is not continuous. Historians are dependent on documents and
these are fragmentary. Of long periods there exist
no records at all, indeed the periods for the history of
which there is any authoritative record are but an
infinitesimal part of the life of mankind; and even
the whole history of mankind is an insignificant incident
in the life of the universe. Then, also, it is true that
of any fragmentary period which some document may
throw into relief, the particular interest to any indi-

vidual may be nil. There is the fact of the event, but the individual interest in it has to be aroused. Are there not then on the one hand documents, bare chronicles, mere records, and on the other hand events with no connexion with our present life? But an event conceived as having no relation to present life would have no historical value. In apprehending it as history at all, we are bringing it into relation with our actual present life. This bringing into relation is not an act of comparison, the discernment of the external resemblance of a particular independent past event to a particular contemporaneous event, it is the actual widening of our apprehension of the present.

This brings us to the other position against which there is a natural prejudice, that all history is contemporaneous history. This means that in thinking the history of the past we bring that past into the present, and not merely is our thinking present, but the history is present history, brought within one present grasp of reality and consciousness of reality. Yet it seems to us that contemporaneous history can only be the consciousness of those events which are themselves unfolding before us in the moment of consciousness and that cut off from that moment, and separated from it completely, are the events which belong to the past. But for true history, as for present consciousness, there is the relation of before and after but no past in the sense of non-existence. In the now of present consciousness, as I have already endeavoured to show, there is no past though there is duration, the duration includes before and after; and what is true of the individual is true also of the universal life, which is history.

" We are accustomed to call any period ' contempo-

raneous history' which we think of as just past—it may
be the last half century, the last decade, the last year or
month or day or even minute. But if we would be
quite precise both in thought as well as speech, we must
only call that history 'contemporaneous' which arises
immediately from the action we happen to be engaged
upon as the consciousness of that action, that is, as the
idea or representation of it. And we should mean by
'contemporaneous' that like every mental act it is
outside time (that is, it is neither before nor after as
everything in a time relation is), it is formed 'at the
same time' as the act with which it is conjoined, and it
is distinguished from that act by a relation which is not
chronological but ideal. Non-contemporaneous or past
history would then be that which, in distinction from
contemporaneous, stands before the mind as formed or
finished, and arises by reflection on history, and whether
the event be a thousand years old or the occurrence
of an hour ago makes no difference.

" Yet, when we look more deeply into the nature of
this history, which we distinguish from contemporaneous
history as being past or non-contemporaneous, we see
that (granting, of course, that it is true history in the
sense that it carries some meaning for us and is not
mere meaningless words) there is no real difference.
Like contemporaneous history, the condition of it is
that the fact from which the history is woven should
vibrate through the historian's soul ; the documents, we
say, must be intelligible. That united or mixed with
the fact there is a story or series of stories of the fact
means only that the fact is presented with more or less
richness, not that it has lost its efficacy which is its
presence. The tales or judgments as they were origin-
ally become themselves facts, documents to be judged

and interpreted. History is never constructed out of narratives but always from documents, or from narratives reduced to documents and treated as such. So that if contemporary history leaps forth from life itself, the history we are accustomed to call non-contemporaneous also springs directly from life, for it is clear that nothing but a present living interest can move us to seek knowledge of a past fact, which fact, therefore, inasmuch as it is drawn forth by a present living interest, responds to a present and not to a past interest. This has been remarked again and again and in a hundred ways in the empirical formulas of historians, and it constitutes the profound meaning of the trite motto *magistra vitae historia*" (Paper read to the Accademia Pontaniana, Nov. 3, 1912).

Contemporaneity, then, is not a character which distinguishes a class of histories from other classes, it is the intrinsic character of every history, and it means that we must conceive the relation of history and life as one of unity, not indeed in the sense of an abstract identity but in that of a synthetic unity wherein are brought together the distinction and the unity of the terms. So understood, the doctrine that all true history is contemporaneous history is no longer a paradox. It underlies the fact we all recognise that no one can ever compose a history of painting who has not seen and enjoyed artistic works; that no one can write a history of philosophy who has no living interest in the works of philosophers; that there cannot be the history of a sentiment such, for instance, as Christian humility, or chivalrous honour, unless there be a capacity to live those particular states of mind. That living interest is not interest in a dead past; it is the past living in our present interest.

Let us now look at the doctrine on its philosophic side. History is not possible without the logical element, and that logical element is the philosophy which conditions history ; but also philosophy is not possible without the intuitive element, and that intuitive element is the history which conditions philosophy.

A philosophical system, or even a philosophical proposition or definition, is as a matter of fact always historically conditioned, inasmuch as it arises in the soul of a particular individual at a particular instant in a particular place and under particular circumstances. And without the historical conditions which call it forth it would not be what it is. The Kantian philosophy could not have appeared in the age of Pericles, because it presupposes, among other things, the exact science of nature which was developed between the Renaissance and the age at which it appeared ; this again presupposes geographical discovery, modern industry, bourgeois or capitalistic civilisation, and so on. It also presupposes the scepticism of Hume, and this in its turn presupposes the deistic principles of the eighteenth century, and these were the result of the English and European religious struggles of the sixteenth and seventeenth centuries, and so on. On the other hand, if Immanual Kant had lived in our day, he could not have written the *Critique of Pure Reason* without such fundamental modifications as would have made it not only another book but a new philosophy, even though his old philosophy should have been contained in it. The philosopher of to-day, however much he may wish to, cannot cast off from him the historical conditions in which he lives, nor can he treat events which have happened as though they had not happened. Those events are bone of his bone, flesh of his flesh, to divest himself of them is impossible. He must take them into

account, he must know historically, and according to
the fulness of his historical knowing is the fulness of his
philosophy.   If he only carries history within him as a
fact of his life and does not also know it, then is he in
no different case from that of the mere animal, and
indeed we ourselves are nothing more when we are
completely immersed in present desire and action.   An
animal is a being, which though conditioned by the
whole of nature and the whole of history, yet does not
know it.   We cannot judge the truth of an answer
unless we understand the meaning of the question, and
so if we would judge the truth of a philosophy we must
know the history (*Logica*, p. 215).

It may be said, of course, that we all recognise this,
for we all agree that a philosopher is a man of learning.
But we are by no means agreed as to the kind or form
of learning which qualifies for philosophy, and it is on
this everything depends.   The form of a philosopher's
learning is, and must be, history.   A philosopher may
be indeed (many would say ought to be) a physiologist,
a mathematician, or a physicist, but the sciences which
these profess are abstractions with no direct relation to
the form of knowledge which is the condition of philosophy.   The philosopher must know the meaning of the
problems of his own time, and how can he know this
unless he knows the problems of the past ?   These
problems may be concerned with the natural and
physical and mathematical sciences, and then he must
know them, not as a specialist, but with the historical
knowledge which enables him to understand the problems
they present to philosophy.   The case of Herbert
Spencer is cited by Croce as an apparent exception
which is really a confirmation of the principle.   Herbert
Spencer, who had read neither Plato nor Kant, yet pro-

duced in eighteen large volumes a system of philosophy which stood for a time to the whole learned world as the representative philosophy of a scientific age. The neglect which has overtaken his work, notwithstanding the great increase in the general interest in philosophy, is, Croce thinks, mainly due to this great defect of historical knowledge. With this judgment there are many among ourselves who agree.

Let us turn, however, from these more popular aspects of the concept of history, which are only illustrative of the philosophical doctrine and useful to show the difficulties and contradictions underlying our ordinary notions, in order to consider the more strictly philosophical meaning. The concept of history is the concept of reality as the eternal present. This is the significance of the two propositions I have considered in their general meaning, viz., first, that every true history is contemporaneous history, and, second, that history and philosophy are identical, philosophy being immanent in history not transcendent to it, as implied in the concept of a philosophy of history. What, then, is the precise meaning of the notion of the eternal present ? What does it imply as to the scope and method of philosophy ?

By eternal is not meant timeless. Many philosophers have distinguished a *species aeternitatis* to which they assign the class of truths which do not depend on the existence of the things about which they are predicated. All necessary propositions, it is said, are eternal ; they are independent of succession in time, and no temporal relations attach to them. The propositions of mathematics, and the entities, such as numbers with which the science of mathematics is concerned, are not existences, and the truth or falsity of propositions concerning them is not dependent on time. They are true for all time and therefore timeless. All existential judgments, on the contrary, are contingent, which means that they refer to the time order. The present is eternal in quite another meaning. It exists and it comprehends existence. The temporal present is a present which succeeds a past and exists by virtue of the non-existence of the past. The eternal present is the present outside which no existence falls. The distinction of past from present is not the distinction of did exist from does exist. The past exists in the present, and the temporal distinctions then and now, before and after, are determinations within existence. It is only the abstractions of the mathematical and natural sciences which have made this doctrine sound contrary to reason. When we reflect on our mind, our life, our self, our individuality, we perceive that what we apprehend as real existence is our past acting in the present. This past is carried along in the present, and cut off from it the present is not the present. Everything which partakes of the nature of life and mind involves in the fact that it is process or activity, the existence of the past in the present. This is the very notion of duration. The eternal present means, therefore, that reality is one duration which includes past, present, and future, as distinct from an abstract present which excludes from itself an abstract past and an abstract future. The concept of history as the eternal present is, then, the affirmation that the past, though determined, exists.

It means, further, that change is both fundamental and universal. This is implied in the doctrine that what we characterise as eternal is present. The present is the continuous process of new creation, the unceasing evolution of new forms. If this be true of reality it will also be true of philosophy, and an important corollary follows in regard to philosophy itself. Philosophy must be a method, not a system. There can be nothing fixed, nothing final in philosophy. The problems of philosophy are never solved in the sense that definite questions are finally and satisfactorily answered. The thought of one age is wholly inadequate to the thought of a succeeding age. Philosophy lives and, like the life it seeks to comprehend, new forms bring with them new problems. A new philosophy is not the re-thinking of an old problem but the emergence of a new problem.

But most important of all in this identity of philosophy with history, and in this concept of history as the eternal present, is that it offers us final and perfect deliverance from the materialistic fallacy. Duration is not the persistence through change of a brute matter, itself alone real, concerning which the questions which arise and the thoughts we have about it are mere phenomena which have their day, die, and leave no trace. History wholly consists in spiritual meaning. Philosophical propositions are indeed historically conditioned, but this does not mean that they are effects deterministically produced by those conditions, they are the creations of the thought which endures in and through them.

Does this infinity of philosophy, this endlessness of the philosophical research, mean that there can be no progress? By no means. The continuous change of philosophy and history is not the unceasing alternation of a making and an unmaking, it is a continual overcoming. The new philosophical proposition is only possible by means of the old, and the old lives eternally in the new which comes forth from it, and also in that other new which is yet again to follow it, and which will turn it, the new now become the old, into another new. In this concept of history, moreover, philosophy itself loses its strict limitations as a special study, becomes adequate to reality, finally merging itself altogether in the history of poetry and literature.

Croce sees a new epoch uprising, an epoch which we cannot delimit because we are in it and of it, but which marks the passing of philosophy from an old concept to a new. The philosophy of the future will be no longer, he thinks, theological, nor metaphysical, nor positivist, it will be historical. The special mark of this new period on which we are entering he would name the new historiography.

" In the philosophy which I have sketched," he says, " Reality is affirmed as Mind, not a mind which stands above the world or runs through the world, but a mind which coincides with the world. Nature is shown to be a moment and product of mind itself. Dualism, therefore (at least that form of dualism which has tormented thought from Thales to Herbert Spencer), is surmounted, and surmounted with it is transcendence whether of a materialistic or of a theological principle. Mind, which is the World, is the mind which is evolving, and therefore it is both one and diverse at the same time, an eternal solution and an eternal problem. The self-consciousness of this mind is the philosophy which is its history or its history which is its philosophy, both substantially one and identical. And the consciousness is identical with the self-consciousness, that is, they are distinct and yet one, like life and thought " (*Storiografia*, p. 286).

The notion which emerges for me from this study of the idea of a new philosophy is that the reality to which I belong, and which I as a self-acting centre view from within, is a universal activity, the most comprehensive term for which is mind. This term expresses better than any other, what no term can express perfectly, both the nature and mode of existence of the universe. It is better than the term life, not because the concept of mind is more than the concept of life, but because it not only implies but wholly includes the concept of life. This activity, mind, manifests itself continuously under two aspects, one static, the other dynamic, the two aspects being in necessary and indissoluble union. We are for ever being determined and determining. These two aspects present themselves to our human outlook in the familiar, homely guise of two concepts, art and history. These two concepts, art and history, apprehended in their rich, concrete, eternally present activity, exhaust reality. What is man ? He is, Croce replies, artist and philosopher.

Yet there seems to cling even to such a reply, understood in its full significance, a theoretical defect. An artist-philosopher is a duality, and no power of thought seems able to arrest the descent of duality into dualism. If there be one main and guiding purpose manifest in Croce's philosophy, it is the persistent effort to find an effective and final escape from the dualism which, first in one form, then in another, confronts the philosopher. May we not say, indeed, that dissatisfaction with final dualism is the intellectual driving force in philosophy from Descartes onward to our own day ? Is, then, dualism really overcome by Croce's method ? With a word on this, which is the alpha and omega of his doctrine, I will conclude this account of the philosophy.

The final and most persistent form in which dualism asserts itself is in the opposition between existence and value, between what is and what ought to be. It appears to stamp as absolute the distinction between mind and nature, for value seems to have a purely spiritual meaning and to be something which mind brings or adds to what it finds already there. Moreover, a certain sense of religious importance attaches to the word "value," and in speaking of it we seem to reach the highest sphere of mind. We saw in the case of art that its lowliness is really its strength, and here also we need to be reminded that the lowliness of value does not detract from its dignity. Value is the essential sign of mind in its lowest manifestation, not something which only comes into view in its highest flights. Yet even in the doctrine that reality is mind, that mind is activity (*dynamicità*), and activity a continual creation of value, it is impossible to escape the opposition between value and a something which is not value but may possess it. Hamlet says, "There is nothing either good or bad, but thinking makes it so." We seem unable to accept this literally. A natural bent of the intellect leads us invariably to interpret it as meaning that there is something indifferent, something neither good nor bad, and that the making it good or bad is a value which thinking has the power to add. Value, then, becomes a judgment opposed to the existential judgment which it presupposes. At once we are brought up on the horns of a logical dilemma. The usual formula of the judgment of value leaves the choice between an absurdity and a tautology. The negative form, "*A* is as it ought not to be," is an absurdity, for if *A* exist it is as it ought to be. On the other hand, the positive form, "*A* is as it ought to be," is a pure tautology, it can only mean that *A* is. And we cannot escape from the dilemma by presupposing a previous judgment on which the judgment " ought " shall depend, as " There exists an *A* so and so determined." To make the judgment of value depend on this previous judgment is to dissipate the very element in the judgment of value which constitutes its special character. This has been illustrated continually throughout our whole exposition. The value of the work of art is not something added to a presupposed existence without aesthetic value. Take away the value and there is no work of art. Again, in history, abstract from the value and it is impossible to find in supposed matter of fact any basis of historical event. There is no unhistorical event which by clothing with historical value the historian can convert into history.

Many philosophers confronted with this dilemma have taken refuge in the view that value is wholly subjective. It must consist, they say, only in feeling, in the individual pleasure or displeasure which accompanies the judgment of existence. But so far from saving the situation this is to make shipwreck of it altogether. This is not Croce's method. Value is not judgment but expression ; instead of value being dependent on existence it is existence which depends on value. The first expression of the intuition is aesthetical and independent of the logical expression. In the simple form of intuition-expression we as yet know no distinction of real and unreal. Yet it is already value. Expression of value Croce describes as the cell of the aesthetic world.

The judgment of reality marks the moment of history. But without the category of value, or rather,

without value as a category or form of mind, judgment
and history are alike impossible. Without knowing
the beautiful, the true, the useful, and the good, there
can be no history, for history is of these values, and
there are no other things.

We are then left with a duality—fact and value,
theoretical and practical reason, thought and action,
mind and nature,—must it give place to dualism ?
" Are knowledge and will, thought and action, two
mental forms parallel and independent one of another
(for this is what dualism means)? Is not the truth,
on the contrary, that thought is thought of action, and
action is action of thought ? Can we conceive pure
intelligence void of will and action ? What would
it think ? Can we conceive blind will and action
void of thought ? What would it do ? There seems
no other way of understanding the two terms except
as distinct and united at the same time and therefore
as opposites, reciprocally positive and negative by turns.
Action is the negation of thought and thought is the
negation of action ; hence the one is not without the
other ; and their duality is not dualism, but dialectic ;
the true unity is not immobility but activity, not pure
being but becoming."

Croce's claim is not to have presented a final system
of philosophy but to have presented a view of philosophy
which finally delivers it from the reproach of a dualistic
hypothesis.

BIBLIOGRAPHY

BENEDETTO CROCE's Italian works are very numerous, and besides philosophy cover a wide range of subjects literary, historical, and political.

The philosophy is contained in a series of four volumes, each complete in itself, but all systematically related. Their general title is "Filosofia dello Spirito." The four volumes are : I. "Estetica come scienza dell' espressione e linguistica generale." II. "Logica come scienza del concetto puro." III. "Filosofia della pratica. Economica ed etica." IV. "Teoria e storia dell**e** storiografia."

The philosophical essays form a special series of three volumes entitled "Saggi filosofici." I. "Problemi di estetica e contributi alla storia dell' estetica italiana." II. "La filosofia di Giambattista Vico." III. "Saggio sullo Hegel, seguito da altri scritti di storia della filosofia."

A small work not included in the above series is "Breviario di estetica." It consists of four lectures on Aesthetic.

"La Critica," a review of literature, history, and philosophy, edited by Benedetto Croce, was started in 1903 and has since been regularly published, appearing bi-monthly. It has contained many of the essays now collected in the above series. In this work Croce is assisted by an able colleague and philosopher of great distinction, Professor Giovanni Gentile of the University of Palermo.

The historical, literary, and political essays have been published in a series entitled "Scritti di storia, letteraria e politica," and of this series there are at present eight volumes. All the above are published by Laterza e Figli of Bari.

The English translations of the philosophical works consist of the following by Mr. Douglas Ainslie : (1) "Aesthetic as Science of Expression and General Linguistic." This is a translation of the first part of "Estetica," which contains the theory of Aesthetic, and there is added a summary of the second or historical part. The volume also contains a translation of the lecture delivered at the General Session of the Third International Congress of Philosophy at Heidelberg in September 1908. It is entitled "Pure Intuition and the Lyrical Character of Art." The original forms part of Volume I. of "Saggi filosofici." (2) "Philosophy of the Practical. Economic and Ethic." This is a translation of the third volume of the "Filosofia dello Spirito." (3) "What is Living and What is Dead of the Philosophy of Hegel." This is a translation of the first and most important of the essays in the third volume of "Saggi filosofici." (4) "Logic as the Science of the Pure Concept." This is announced but has not appeared at the time of writing. All the above are published by Macmillan & Co.

Mr. Ainslie's translations of the philosophy, particularly the "Aesthetic" and the "Philosophy of the Practical," have met with rather severe criticism on the ground that they leave the philosophy somewhat obscure. I do not think, however, that this is due to any want of accuracy in the rendering, it is rather due to an over-conscientiousness in the translator, which leads him to preserve the *ipsissima verba* of the author, and to introduce neologisms of doubtful value. Mr. Ainslie has offered a spirited defence of his method in his prefaces, and it is certainly due to him to acknowledge that he was the first to recognise the originality of the new philosophy and to introduce the author to English readers. The general recognition may lead Mr. Ainslie to give us a complete revision of his first two translations in a new edition.

There is an English translation of Volume II. of the "Saggi filosofici"—"The Philosophy of Giambattista Vico." Translated by R. G. Collingwood and published by Howard Latimer. This is a work of great interest for its history as well as for its philosophy.

There is also an English translation of a book entitled "Historical Materialism and the Economics of Karl Marx." The translation is by C. M. Meredith with an Introduction by A. D. Lindsay, published by Howard Latimer. This appeared in 1914. There is no work of Croce in Italian with this title, and the book appears to consist of a selection of critical notices of various books contributed to Reviews between 1895 and 1900. They are, therefore, all earlier than the "Filosofia dello Spirito." The book presents, in fragmentary and occasional form, some of the doctrines, particularly the relation of economics to ethics and the theory of history, which are incorporated in the "Filosofia della pratica."

One of the articles in "Encyclopaedia of the Philosophical Sciences. Vol. I. Logic" (Macmillan & Co., 1913) is contributed by Croce. It is entitled "The Task of Logic."

A short personal account and bibliography of the two Italian philosophers whom Croce regards as his predecessors—Vico and De Sanctis—will be useful to the student. They are continually referred to in Croce's writings.

Giambattista Vico was born at Naples on June 23, 1668, and died on January 23, 1744. After his university course he became tutor in a private family, a situation which he occupied for nine years and which gave him the opportunity of study. In 1697 he obtained the Professorship of Rhetoric at the University of Naples, a post he held for thirty-six years. The annual stipend was very small—one hundred ducats (equivalent to about £17)—but he married, and managed by private lessons and literary work to support his family. His early works are : "De ratione studiorum" (1708) ; "De antiquissima Italorum sapientia" (1710) ; "De universi juris uno principio et fine uno" (1720) ; "De constantia jurisprudentis" (1721). The work on which his fame rests is "Principii d' una scienza nuova." The first edition was published in 1725, the second edition, with so many additions as to make it practically a new work, in 1730. The "New Science" is the science of history. One Book of the second edition, entitled "The Discovery of the True Homer," at once attracted to it the attention of the contemporary learned world.

Croce's works on Vico, besides the volume of the "Saggi filosofici" already noticed, are : "Bibliografia Vichiana," "Le fonti della gnoseologia Vichiana." He has also edited : "G. B. Vico : L' Autobiografia, il carteggio e le poesie varie."

Francesco de Sanctis was born in 1817. He was a private schoolmaster at Naples when, in 1848, he was suddenly arrested and confined in the prison of the Castel dell' Uovo. He was afterwards exiled. He lectured first in Turin and then in Zürich. After the expulsion of the Bourbons he returned to Naples. He was appointed Minister of Education in the new United Kingdom of Italy by Cavour in 1861. In 1866 he dropped out of public life. He died in 1881. His chief work is, "Storia della letteratura italiana," two volumes. The notes of his university lectures are being published by Croce in "La Critica."

INDEX OF NAMES

DATE DUE